Artist of Life

Festival of Youth

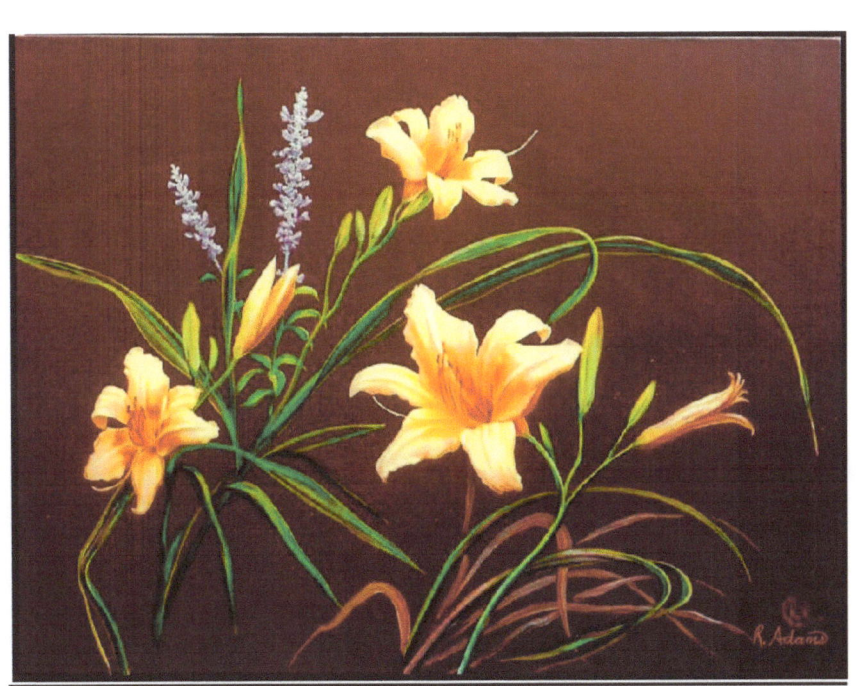

Printed in the United States of America
First Printing 2016
ISBN 978-0-692-70441-7
The Shining Light Press Roger Adams

Introduction: The Festival of Youth

When I first met Reverend Saito in 1963 (I was 27 at the time) he was already in the process of creating a festival for the younger set at the church where I attended. These were the Junior Busei's, the younger generation of temple members, who he was in charge of as assistant minister. His job was to gather and create a festival that would not only involve them but also to appeal to the older generation of parents and church members who could also gather a teaching that would inspire them as well. Thus the festival took on the title of: "Artist of Life".

To do this he borrowed from three sources: his own teacher, Reverend Haya Akegarasu, Miozawa Kenji, and the author of a play, "The Twilight Crane", by Junji Kinoshita. All of them expressed their life as their own art. Therefore, with these three he composed a festival along with a booklet which he used as a focal point to expose these first two teachers' teaching plus the story line from the play itself. It was quite a production in which many people were involved from different directions that were also included. He also needed a poster which he asked me to do in order to advertise the event. I created a poster that I printed in silk screen, and he filled in the Japanese part. Altogether we worked many hours on the project - to such an extent that towards the end we were sleep deprived way into the night passed our bedtime, taking care of all the details necessary to bring it to a success. At that time I also met Joan Sweany (who later became his secretary) and was our director in charge of seeing to it that we became good actors to take part in the stage production.

The gist and meaning of the story is that, I, who played the part of Yohyo, a simple farmer who saved the life of a crane that was shot with an arrow by a hunter. To thank him she turned into a beautiful young woman who then became Tsu. They fell in love and got married. Then she, out of her love and gratitude for him, and after he had gone asleep, wove a beautiful garment out of golden feathers (a kin-han'e kimono). Then as she was weaving this garment late at night by candle light, a villager happened to pass by and saw what she was making through an open window. Surprised by what he saw he spoke of this to his friend, another greedy villager, and the both of them came up with a plan that the both of them decided was a good opportunity to get rich. They then had to convince both her and her husband Yohyo of selling what she had made and turn it into a profit. But she refused.

Feeling as she did for doing it out of her love for Yohyo she could never consent to such a thing. But they did convince her husband who then insisted that she produce more of these garments - together they could become rich! She, hearing this, backed off. But he became more and more persistent, even accusing her that she didn't love him enough by taking feathers out of her own body to weave into a golden kimono. It became too much for her to take, and so one day during the twilight hours she decided to leave him. She transformed herself back into a crane and flew away. He, seeing her flying away ran after her, anxiously shouting, "Come back! Come back!" but it was to no avail.

In such tears, he realized his terrible mistake and stumbling to the ground shouted: "What have I done?" It was if he fell into the abyss which was like hell. The flames that consumed his mind, body, and soul appeared as hot burning tears. As he arose from these flames he gained a new life. Then in an instant she miraculously appeared before him, and they were once again reunited as husband and wife. Hugging each other they expressed their love for each other as the final scene ends and the curtain falls.

*   *   *

Reverend Akegarasu's "Brilliancy of the burning self!" was in an article that he wrote in which he expressed: "Flames of total cremation of self is my only enlightenment." It was the result of an incident that happened with a nurse who was taking care of him at the time. News got out of this incident, even though small, was carried out of proportion, and as a result it ruined his reputation as a reputed lecturer on the Buddhist Dharma. Adding to that, he was accused of betraying the movement that his teacher, Reverend Kiozowa, established. As a result he was abandoned, abused, and left alone.

When he read about this revelation in a religious "scandal sheet" he felt the flames of hell befall him. In his article he describes this, which is difficult for us to understand. Prior to this incident he was a most respected speaker and lecturer on the Buddhist Dharma, believed to be following the footsteps of his teacher as he went around gathering numerous numbers of followers throughout Japan. He was popular on the list of reputed teachers. Yet he was not really coming up with his own life, a life that would turn him into a devil.

But then it happened about the news of this incident. He was   immediately sent into hell. While in hell he became this devil who saw himself as the devil, and within the flames itself he arose to shine like that of the phoenix arising from the flames to gain a new life. Out of this new life we have the best articles written by him that shows what the Buddha-Dharma really feels like. He penetrates into my being like no other. He enlightens - as he speaks to me directly and so I feel a true dialogue with a person I totally trust and respect.

That which goes beyond gratitude emerges - that of my teacher Reverend Gyoko Saito who was the one who presented this "Festival of Youth" at a time when I first entered the Buddhist teaching and who right away gave me the proper direction by showing me that I was like Yohyo, the simple farmer who turned into such a greedy person as the person most likely to play the part of what I was.

R.Adams
3/25/2016

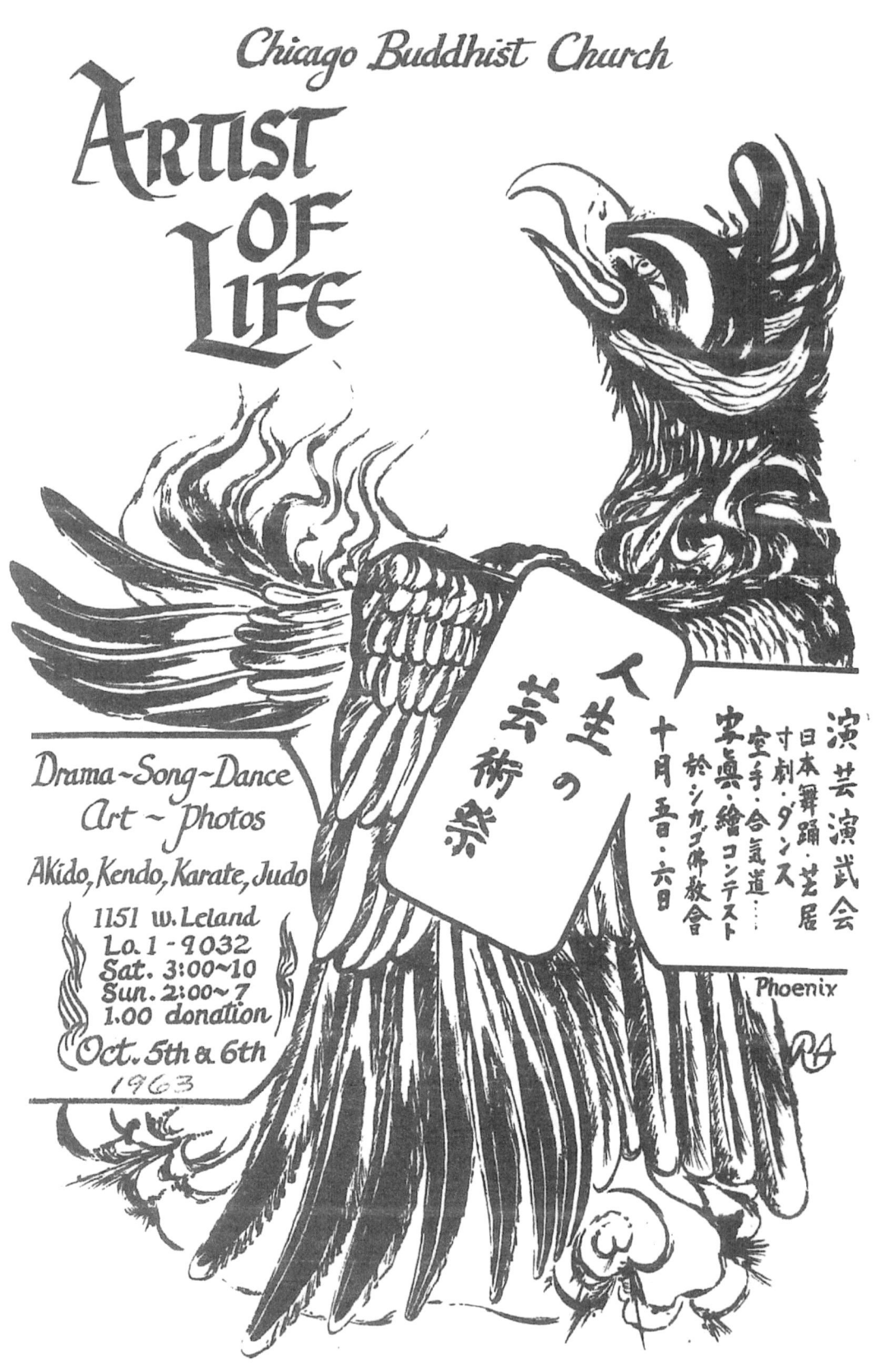

Chicago Buddhist Church

ARTIST OF LIFE

Drama ~ Song ~ Dance
Art ~ Photos

Akido, Kendo, Karate, Judo

1151 W. Leland
Lo. 1 - 9032
Sat. 3:00 ~ 10
Sun. 2:00 ~ 7
1.00 donation
Oct. 5th & 6th
1963

人生の芸術祭

演芸演武会
日本舞踊・芝居
寸劇・ダンス
空手・合気道…
写真・繪コンテスト
於シカゴ佛教會
十月五日・六日

Phoenix

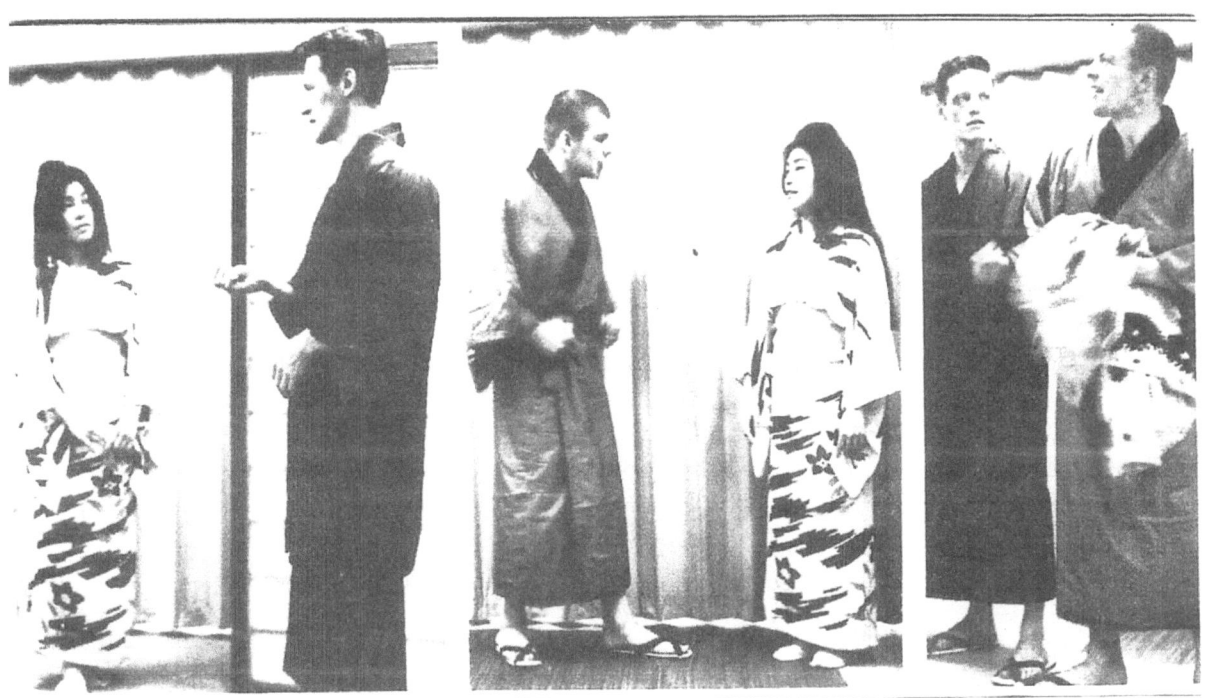

"The Twilight Crane"

By Junji Kinoshita

Junji Kinoshita's "Twilight Crane" is among the best-known of modern Japanese plays. It is based on the old legend of the crane wife.

A simple young farmer saves the life of a crane, which has been wounded by a hunter's arrow. Later the crane turns into a beautiful young woman and comes to the farmer to thank him. They fall in love and are married. As the play opens, the two are living happily together in the middle of the wide countryside ••••••••

Cast

IN ORDER OF APPEARANCE

YOHYO a simple young farmer	ROGER ADAMS
CHILDREN from the village	DEANNA & MARK HIGASHI
TSU Yohyo's wife	FRANCIS HASHIGUCHI
SODO a greedy villager	CARL SMITH
UNZU another greedy villager	MITSURI

Directed by Joan Sweany

Artist of life

"Brilliancy of the burning self! These flames of hell blaze up seize earth, are about to invade heaven -- no ledge to put my foot on, no cave to hide my body in, and no refuge for my soul! All havens, all old friends, are horribly consumed in these hellish flames. My adored God and Buddha, in the high heavens, melt in these deep fires of hell.

"For a long time I tried to kill the flames, I tried to escape them. I ran to persons, I ran to things. I prayed to God and Buddha, reciting Nembutsu, trying to get power. All in vain.

"Then, at every instant, the monstrous fires assailed me. I crouched in silence, I jumped on anguished screams. But always I was straining with the wish, "I don't want to burn, I don't want to die!" while the raging flames advanced upon my legs and arms and reached my head.

"I was not aware of it but I stood in these flames like the lord of the fire.

"Now the burning had covered my whole body, has reached and seized my soul. Anguish! "I am now <u>it</u>!" Shouting this, I hurl myself into the flames. Strangely, at this moment, I gain a new life.

"Spirit of burning, radiant with the flames of hell. Spirit of Quietude, shining throughout all worlds and space! Now moving on emboldened, without regret or fear, without thought or qualm, with only this burning of the fires of hell, I overgrow the entire universe.

"No man gains a new life unless he dreads the fire that will consume his body and soul, unless he mourns its coming. But no man knows Enlightenment unless he surrenders to this fire of suffering.

"Flames of the total cremation of self are my only enlightenment."

In the above article Reverend Akegarasu said, "Flames of the total cremation of self are my only enlightenment." Without understanding this, there is no Buddhism in action; there is only organization, only the business world.

What is Buddhism in action? It is not rules, it is not organization, it is not Authorized Teachings. It comes out of enlightenment.

We are human beings. Each of us is the self center of all ego, regardless of youth or age. "Artists of life," which is the theme of the youth festival, expresses this teaching of Reverend Akegarasu, which is the basic teaching of Buddhism.

- Reverend Gyoko Saito

Festival of youth

The Youth Co-ordinating Council started working on the Festival of Youth at the beginning of this year, but the original inspiration for the festival comes out of a short article written in 1926 by Miyazawa Kenji, a well known Japanese poet and a pupil of Reverend Akegarasu. Kenji grew up in the very poor farming country of northern Japan. As a teacher in the agricultural high school he witnessed the poverty and near - desperation of the students and their parents. He felt the lack of purpose in the lives of these people. What he faced there in the young farmers' problems was much deeper and more difficult than what we all face today. Miyazawa Kenji, became a farmer himself, giving up all his intellectual interests to live with the farmers as one of them.

The following excerpts from Kenji's article express his feeling about the art of the farmer's life. This article and its results are a manifestation of the spirit of Reverend Akegarasu's teachings:

"What is the art of living? It is simply this: An expression of cosmic feeling--through the earth, through people, and through individuality. And the way of creation, whether conscious or unconscious, *is* to affirm real life all the time, while all the time heightening and deepening our experience of it. This makes life and nature into a continuous beautiful photograph and poem, a great drama and dance. This is how we should think about and enjoy nature and our own lives. This art helps us communicate with each other, and brings all of society to the same feeling, and finally brings all beings to the Ultimate.

"What do we mean by artist? The idea of professional artist should die--everyone should feel as an artist does. Everyone should be free to let his inner mind speak to him, and everyone is an artist when he does this. Then, if an inspiration comes to us, we throw all our energies into it. Then, no matter who we are, everyone is drawn to us to support us. When our inspiration passes, we return to our ordinary life: but we can stand on our own feet. Here, then, are many truly free artists. Unique billions of geniuses live together in one world: Earth is heaven.

"Oh my friends, shall we combine our rightful powers to make a huge four-dimensional art within our own lives and in our fields and gardens? First of all, let us scatter ourselves all over the sky as bits of the brightening cosmos. At the same time, we go on living our own lives. This place we stand in *is* the sun of our universe; the surrounding land is its solar system; and our country is the whole great galaxy of stars.

MY SPIRIT IS DANCING

Snow is covering up everything and falling more and more. On the fallen snow the wind blows sharply, so cold that it almost breaks the skin. But my mind is burning. The snow storm rages so terribly that it whips the world into a gray mist. But my mind is shining.

Once, I would cry over the novels of Turgenev, I would be taken out of myself by the novels of De Maupassant. Submerged in the darkness of the world, I cried, reciting the Nembutsu in a sorrowful voice. But now I have thrown away that Nembutsu. The mind that was seeking the light is broken, I myself shine out. In the darkness of the abyss, my mind alone burns and shines. I ask no agreement from the majority, no cooperation from society. Regardless of what they call me--dangerous thinker or outcast--my mind is too hot and too shining: They cannot cool it off with abuse.

****

In the cemetery now, the spring wind has come. Look there: On the cold tombstone the green moss flowers! A bush-warbler is singing, and the song almost bursts his throat. Even that old woman with deep wrinkles on her face is humming a song quietly to herself. Listen to the young love song sung by the old wrinkled woman-- look, and feel it.

New grasses are pushing up from under the fallen leaves. Let's listen to the true voice, coming from a great distance, whispering so close to the ear, and from very deep down, telling us so loudly: "Let us live, all of us, Let us burn up everything. Let us shine.

"Look at it all! That sun, those stars , the ocean and the mountains and rivers and ponds, the grasses and trees and people, the animals, and birds, the insects, tea kettles, the blankets, ink, the pens! Everything is shedding tears, whatever we see, under the heavens and on all the earth. And each teardrop burns—doesn't it?—and shines.

"Nothing is hard enough to resist these molten tears. No power is stronger than these tears, none can overcome them. Look around you! Molten tears shining reverently—can't you see them?"

I listen to that deep voice. I look at those shining tears. No wonder I cannot help dancing. No wonder I can't help feeling power. My muscles will spring to action with a touch.

⁂ ⁂ ⁂ ⁂ ⁂ ⁂ ⁂ ⁂

In front of the Tsuruga-oka-hachiman temple, the lady Shizuka danced, singing, "O Shizu! O Shizu! I want to change this terrible time back to the old days when my husband was with me and happy with me.

"Shizu, Shizu, Shizu!" she repeated, "I want to change my whole life—but no way to change the present for the old days."

She says this in the presence of her enemy, Minamoto Yopitoma, her husband's own brother but the heal of an army that is pursuing him. She is not afraid of Minamoto, but look at the shining tears that drop; feel the power that overflows in her voice. All those who look at her and hear her, melt into this and become silent. No power, no sword can conquer this.

     Shizuka Gozen, dance! This dance is so serious that no opportunist, no flirt could dance it. O my Shizuka Gozen, my soul goes back seven hundred years and is dancing with you. Your dance lives seven hundred years later, and you are dancing my dance with me. Those who understand nature through books, those who solve life by thinking-- how can they comprehend my dance and yours? How glad I am to dance such a powerful dance! I am so joyful that I touch the edge of tears.

✻ ✻ ✻ ✻ ✻ ✻ ✻ ✻ ✻

     When I was young I saw the play called <u>Shussekagekyo.</u> The hero Kagekyo is lover of the dancer Akoya. The hero's enemy, Hatakeyama Shizetada, in pursuit of him, captures the beautiful dancer Akoya and makes her reveal, by means of a song sung to the music of the samisen, place of her lover. And the samisen music begins....

     That play, that tragedy, I have never forgotten to this day.
The tears shining in Akoya's eyes, the samisen plucked by her fingers, the tone of her voice--in these you find the manifestation of indescribable soul and unlimited authority.
How is it a fickle and wanton woman can have such sorrow, tears so full of authority? How can she have such song and music? Who can refrain from crying, singing, playing this music with her? Aching, sympathizing, shedding tears. My hands of their own accord came together in reverence, so serious my feeling, seeing this play.

Let my life harmonize with Akoya's samisen music and her singing. Longed-for Akoya! Your tears absorb my soul. May the strength of your sorrow become all of myself.

* * * * * * * * *

O Shizu! O Akoya! Your soul's burn with love knowing you cannot have it, yet hoping and shin- ing. Tears burst out from this, song overflows from this, and dance springs up from this.
  Without having this single-minded spirit, this indomitable spirit; where are the shining tears? Without this spirit where can we hear
the burning voice? Without this, where can we see the dance that shakes the earth?

* * * * * * * * *

Spring comes--spring is here. The flowers are unfolding and birds sing. My soul is dancing out into the whole universe which is as small as a little room.

February 16, 1917 Reverend Haya
Akegarasu (Translated 1963
G. Saito, J. Sweany)

Inspiration within Life Itself R. Adams 2/27/2016

What is my art? My art is to capture the beauty of nature. So in that sense nature is my focal point. Within nature there are an infinite number of points, always moving, always changing. By being at one with nature I can visualize this eternal movement within my own life. By expressing it using the various tools that I have at my disposal, along with the various ways of seeing it, I can flow as nature flows and accomplish my wish of portraying the spiritual life of the will and the spirit that nature exhibits as life itself. This infinite variety of life becomes a focal point for my own life. I am made happy as I direct my attention to the beauty and simplicity of nature. What a subject matter I have to work with! It is endless. The starting point of creation of natures' wish is within my own creation.

We are all experiencing creation even within our own bodies. Our own bodies are being created right now, as the number of cells within our body is constantly being created as they are being replenished on a continuous basis just as in all of sentient life; so we too, are of natures' embracing spirit. Feeling it this way makes me exclaim: Ah, natural man! So now we can see that being at one with nature clearly and distinctly changes our perspective and makes us realize the infinite transition that takes place within our own mind; that is, from stasis and a fixed understanding, to a living, fresh understanding that awakens to life itself.

And within this living essence of life comes the shout of my being as I taste it and as it comes up with an expression as my very own art. In this case I lose the "I" in the wondrousness of the world – lose myself to find the true essence of my being: I as I. The selfless natural world penetrates into the depths of my being as I am in the process of learning from a teaching that goes beyond words that directly penetrates into my being. This is what is known as the shout of nature which unfolds as the living reverberation that I wish to capture using the various tools such as brushes, paint and canvas; or structure, composition, color, shape and form which I can bring together to create the art that inspires me.

This is the living source behind the transitions that simply happen and come to me by way of flowers, landscapes, or whatever there is that captures my attention in the immediacy of the moment. Thus, the art that I practice comes from the oneness I feel towards all of life that speaks to me directly and beautifully. As such, all others are directly involved in a one-world movement that I can contribute to and share with others.

So in that sense my job is to beautify the world, and with a clarified mind makes this direction truly fulfilling to my own life which I want to share and to give generously. Love and warmth are given to me as I go about my work with effort and single-mindedness. Some difficulties - even the seeming impossible - are gratefully transcended in this fullness of life!

We have a garden within ourselves. Amazing! The soil for this garden is within our very life itself. The soil is within our own mind. From this rich soil new things are born, new shoots pop up. They grow, they bloom, and they fulfill their life. That's why we were born - to fulfill our lives! Emptiness inspires life as this is our garden. With an open mind listen to those things which can contribute to and fertilize our garden. For then you are like nature in all its simplicity and creation. The feeling of being embraced by life itself comes by way of life itself.

Within this spirit there is the will, and the will goes forward to produce life. Now I'm at one with nature as nature flows as a natural person. True happiness follows this, as my deepest wish is being fulfilled. This feeling for the spiritual life comes that I can nurture and cultivate.

We can get stale and moldy if we stay in one place too long. So we always have to push forward no matter what. Our art then becomes an artist of life, in which everything we do is an expression of it. An artist of life is not merely concerned with being an artist, for there are no labels that describe the kind of art that an artist of life does. Thus he does not take pride in the fact that he, being such-and-such an artist, is someone special, different, or superior to others who don't have the same ability that he does, but just being an ordinary person who follows the way.

The way is: even though I paint, I am not an artist. Even though I may write poetry, I am not a poet. Even though I may write music or play music, I'm just being myself doing what I like to do. I cannot accept a category that defines the self itself as an entity as separate from others, considered as something special. This is so often overlooked as we go about labeling things and people connecting their work from who they really are in terms of being a human being. I hate to be separated from others by labels that judge so-and-so as "artist", "poet", "musician", or whatever it is we do. These terms do not fit to who I really am as I am this subtle self of the boundless life of not knowing how to define myself.

We start out admiring flowers, and seek a way to describe their beauty, and so we set out to describe their essence that we've received. But have we ourselves become this flower that we so admire? How can I not feel it?

Being just an observer to life is not life. So often we become like scholars and philosophers, who think and observe life two-dimensionally without any real feeling for a subject point, and without a space and time dimension. We try to figure life out through our relative wisdom and so we get entangled in so much round-about thinking which remains untouched by an organic understanding. An organic understanding follows nature's way of non-discrimination and non-interference. Throw away the former and get into the latter, in a four-dimensional world that is moving like that of nature – indeed, just like our own bodies do! You know, how we interpret life depends on how we jump into it and express it.

Flowers, for example, burst though their buds with such power and within such single-mindedness fulfilling their wish to open to the sun or the light that beckons them to bloom enabling them to fulfill their deepest wish. So too, when we, expressing our deepest wish, expose ourselves as being naked before life itself. Why can't we be our naked selves instead of wearing so many artificial coverings? We like to label ourselves with titles while wearing these artificial masks that are as ornaments used to enhance ourselves while covering up our not-so-nice or deficient side.

Our organic spirit is constantly moving and changing which is the reality of impermanence, and is the basis of Buddhism. As the blood in our bodies circulate throughout our body, so too does our spirit in association with this organic and physical process that exist as truth, the wisdom of Prajna, which means intuitive wisdom. Intuitive wisdom is a matter of our intellect.

Beyond that is the mind that sets up a manner of logic into blocks which are used to figure out life in a scholarly manner. The scholarly life-style is cold, like cold feet!. Here, we think of things objectively. But through our oneness with nature we see things subjectively. Here we see the wisdom as to the intuitive nature of the spirit through the eyes of an awakened person. I can't help seeing the changes going on within the life as exemplified by nature and within the spirit of naturalness, life itself is given to me - like the very first buds of spring!

Life can be difficult, and within that difficulty plunge forward bravely, courageously, and by doing so experience the brightness that life gives. In this brightness of life, our religion is carried forth by this "onceness" or "isness" that pushes me forward into a dimension that includes the sun, the moon, and the stars of the infinite; which includes a sense of universal brotherhood whereas I can touch the lives of all others, universally. This is what is meant by artist of life: Come up with your own life as your own art.

Production, living production, is what has drawn me, and continues to draw me into the great unknown and unknowable resource of creation itself. Listen it says, listen only to that essence of your life and you shall be free to express it in any form as your own true shout!

*   *   *   *

How much does our early karma's effect our future development and personality? When I was at the age of five my mother was killed in an auto accident in which I was also involved. The conditions were such that I was put in an orphanage as my father could not take care of me alone. But I remember my original mother as hugging and embracing me. Eleven years later my father remarried and together with my step-mother we settled in a old house they purchased. Seeing that I was doing artwork she encouraged it and enrolled me in the Children's School at the Art Institute of Chicago and the Field Museum of Chicago (both connected). This exposure widened my perspective as to the various cultures of the world when I was just thirteen to fifteen years old. From then on I was set in the direction to become a student of art, which altogether began to influence me through a world-wide view of humanity through its culture and religion. Later in my college years, I won a scholarship to attend the School of The Art Institute of Chicago, so again I was exposed to all the world's cultures through its art. Through this one-world exposure I got to see the world through a different perspective which went beyond the conventional, normal, young adult experience.

In terms of religion the orphanage was Protestant, but since my step-mother was Catholic, I was raised as a Catholic and sent to a Catholic grammar school. But since both of these left no real impression on me I was left open to explore a different way in thinking about spirituality in painting from nature; which stimulated my desire when the time came, to seek an unknowable essence about myself, a spiritual direction that eventually led me to Buddhism in the early sixties. What I really needed was a religion that touched my life, which I got when I soon met with the teacher. I remember his words: "I love you. Why don't you love me?" This kind of amazed me, but his expression was one of embracing a true dialogue.

This is important, for what I was really seeking was the truth about my life. Something that really touched me and created in me a desire to follow it and listen to it. Then through the process of deepening of one's life, there were many ways of expressing it. One way was through the various artworks that I was inspired to do; and, inheriting a house with a garden it was only natural that my own back-yard was included, along with so many other places.

My teacher once told me that my job was to beautify the world, and so I am including various art works that I've done throughout the years and included some of them in this book. I hope that you enjoy my production, as I'm happy to include them. Although I never intended it, by capturing the beauty of nature and natural life, I, in the process felt its living essence penetrate into my life, whereas my life became like an artist of life; and, in drawing inspiration from the early teaching I received in the temple where I took my first steps into the Buddha-Dharma. How fortunate I've been to have as the teacher, Reverend Gyoko Saito.

Artist of Life: Art of the Brush

*Be the sun of your own kingdom, the kingdom of one is many, many is one.

*Arising out of its own cocoon the butterfly is sunning itself. Breaking free, it has fulfilled its life in transforming itself to rest among the lotus flowers.

*"Wealth does not satisfy nor does poverty quench." But the free person is allowed to soar into the spacious skies unhindered by worldly things that would only bind him down and/or block his view. He is richly rewarded beyond compare in the world of freedom. In the world of work and play he enjoys an ordinary life in a real effort to live his life fully, so he doesn't feel cramped, tight, and stingy in the poverty stricken mind of the isolated person. His life is full, and in this fullness he gives to others. He, feeling such a wish, gives to those who are misguided and the lonely of the world. Through the true riches of life itself he doesn't need the artificial life-style of accumulation through greed. The true riches of life are brought to him without intentionally seeking them. This is the feeling that in such reverence brings together the hands in worship to the essence of life that can bring the emergence of tears. For within its compassion it kills you, for it kills the separation between you and the other. Then it comes as the embracing spirit of life itself. This is all I need to replenish myself, drinking from the waters of natural life.

*Following the way is not difficult because of its simplicity and clarity. But what is difficult is attachment to self – the most difficult, and final attachment.

*Buddha-consciousness is following the life of freshness. The flower just beginning to open is this freshness. Already opened it is beginning to fade. We should seek the life within ourselves that is just beginning to open. This is where the truth pops-up unexpectedly that doesn't have my control over it. It just comes through natural means as it breaks through the barriers of accepted logical and conventional thinking, while opening up the doors and windows of our mind. The sparks of creation!

*Think of the light-house that guides ships through the treacherous waters of life. Then think of the light-house called the Buddha–Dharma. It provides the light that enlightens the darkest aspects of our mind. It bends the unbending. It refurbishes the old. It breathes life into the sick. And because it is living, we who are students and listeners who hear the teaching gain our life and awaken from the dead and half-dead existence. Throw out the useless and futile existence of the intellect that thinks it can solve life's problems. For the storehouse of knowledge is within you and is the lighthouse of the bright light that says: "Come as you are. I will protect you. Don't hesitate, don't look to the right, don't look to the left, but go straight forward no matter what happens, and diligently seek the way."

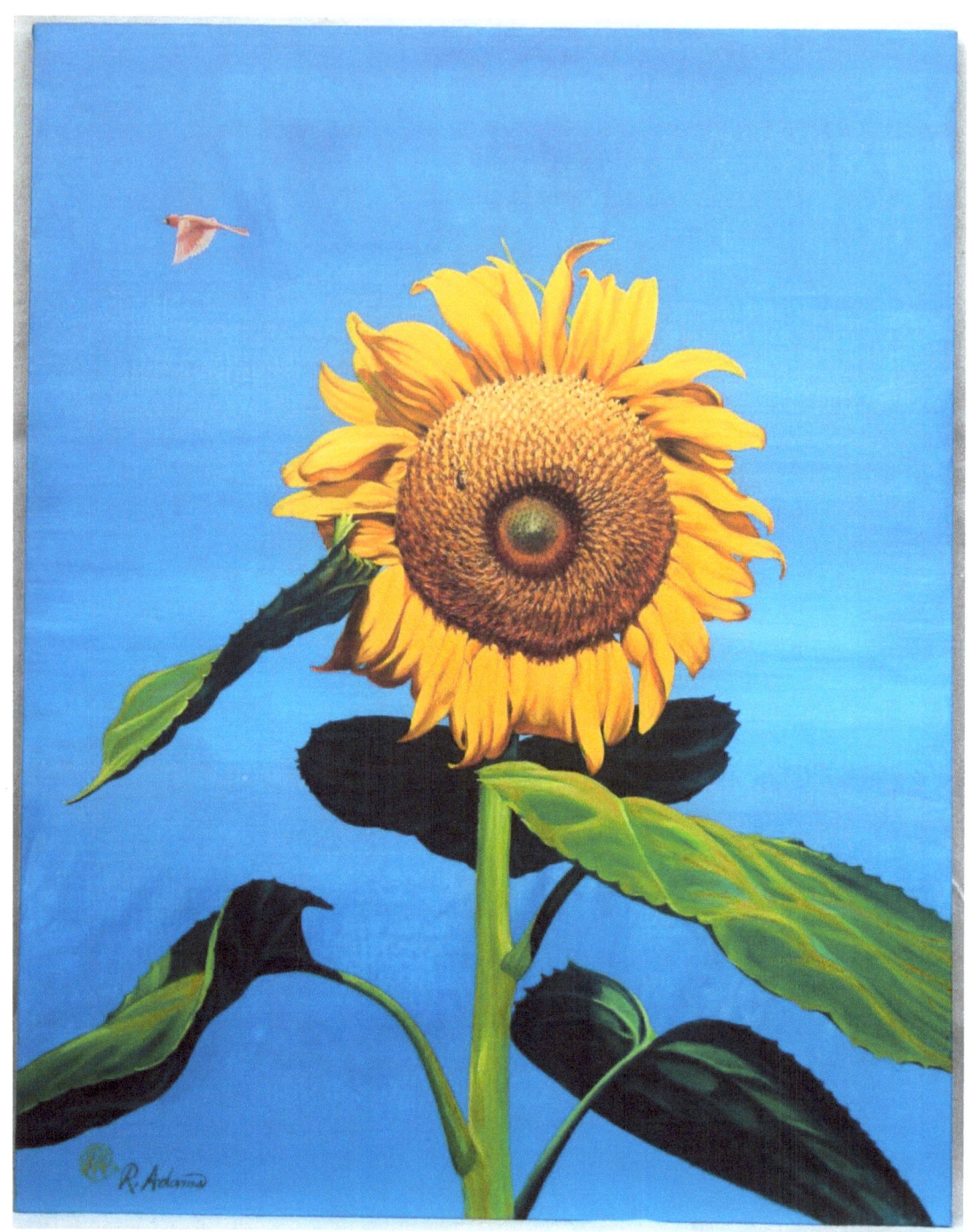

"Sunrise"

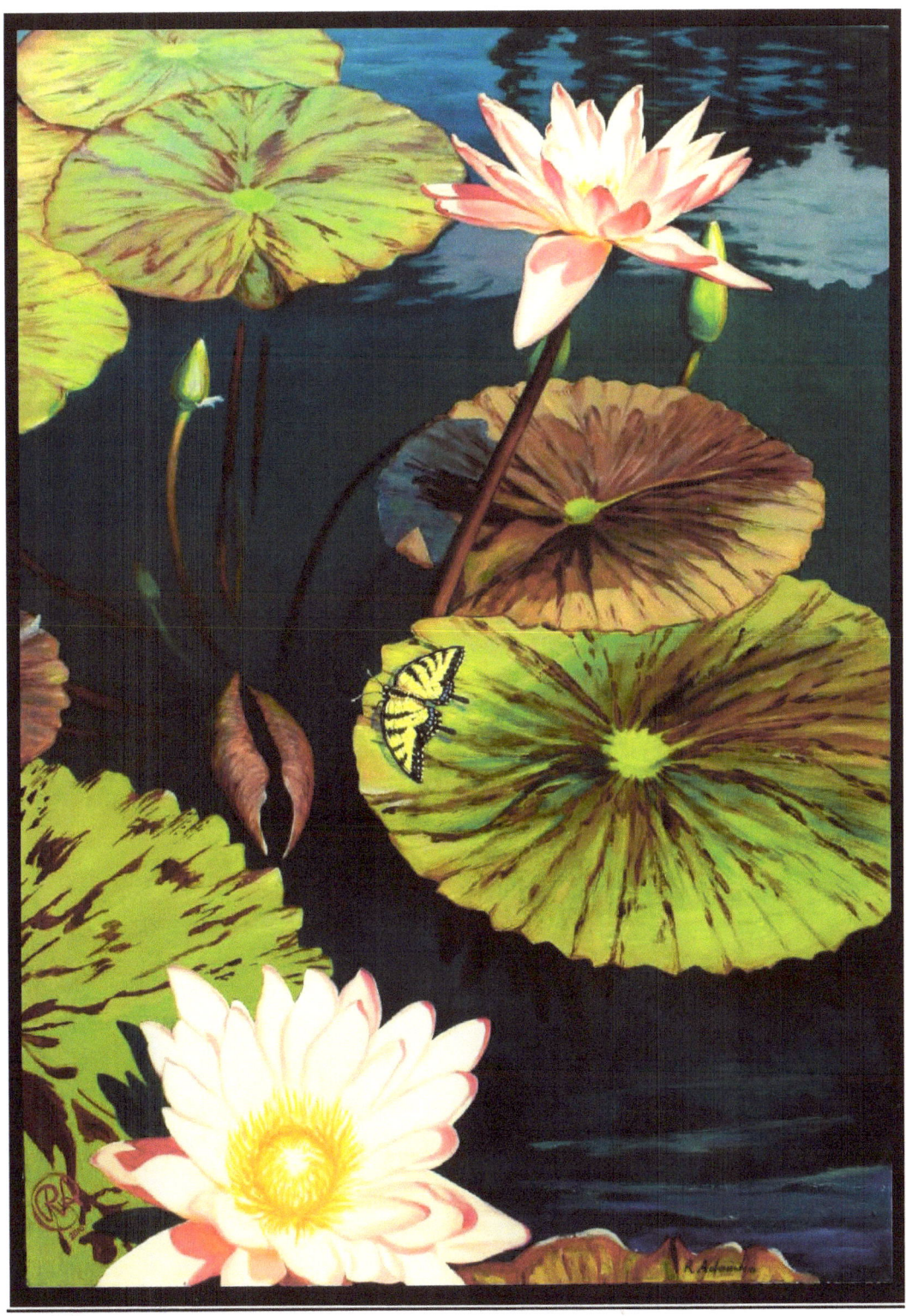

"Among The Lotus"

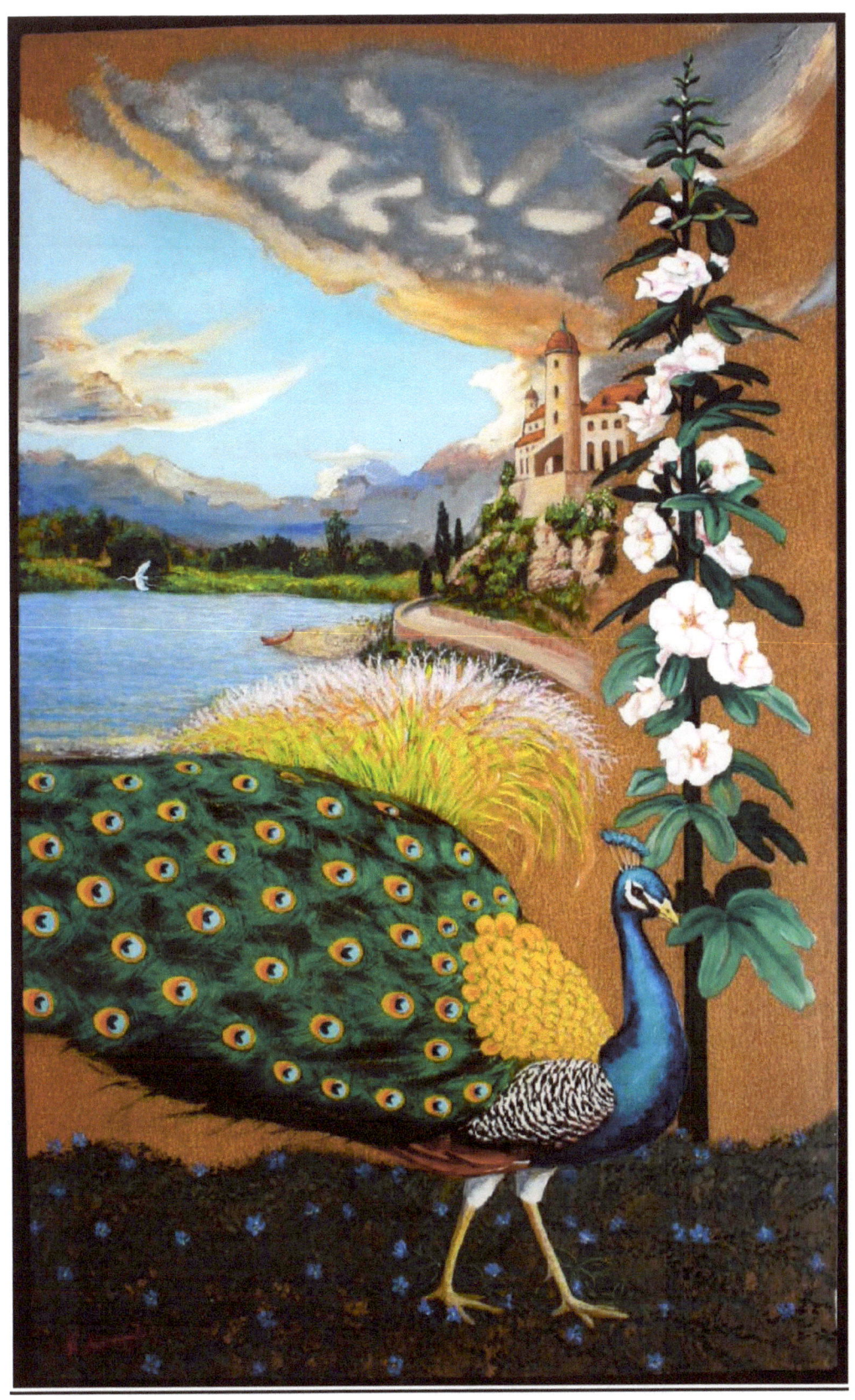

"The Peacock"

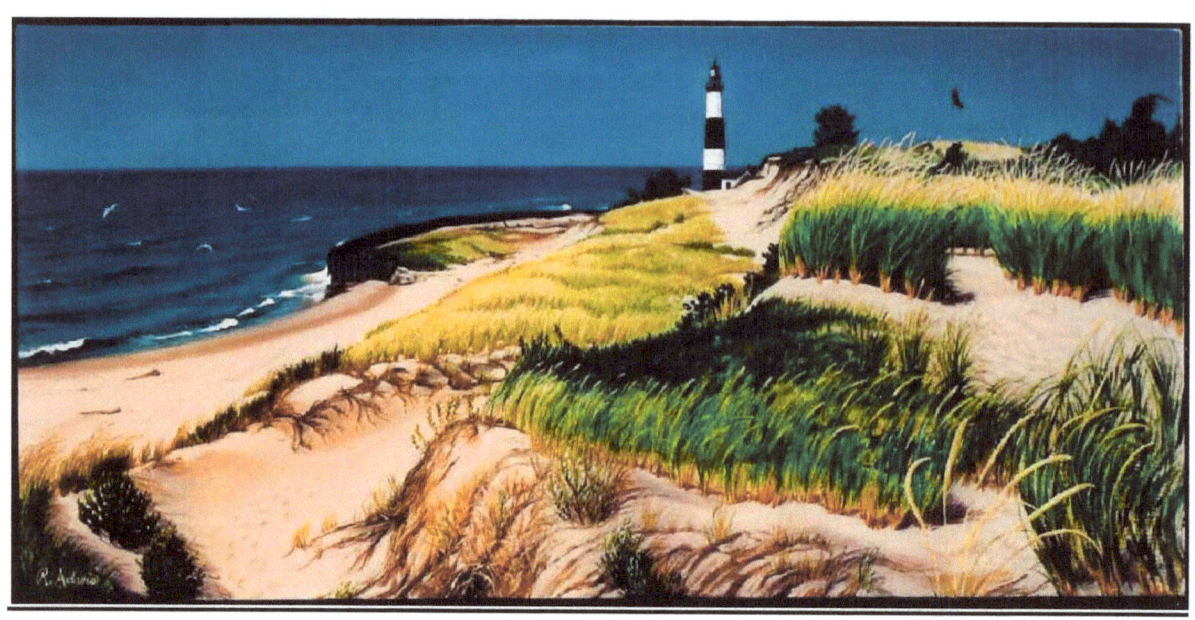

"Flowing Grasses"

"Fresh Breezes"

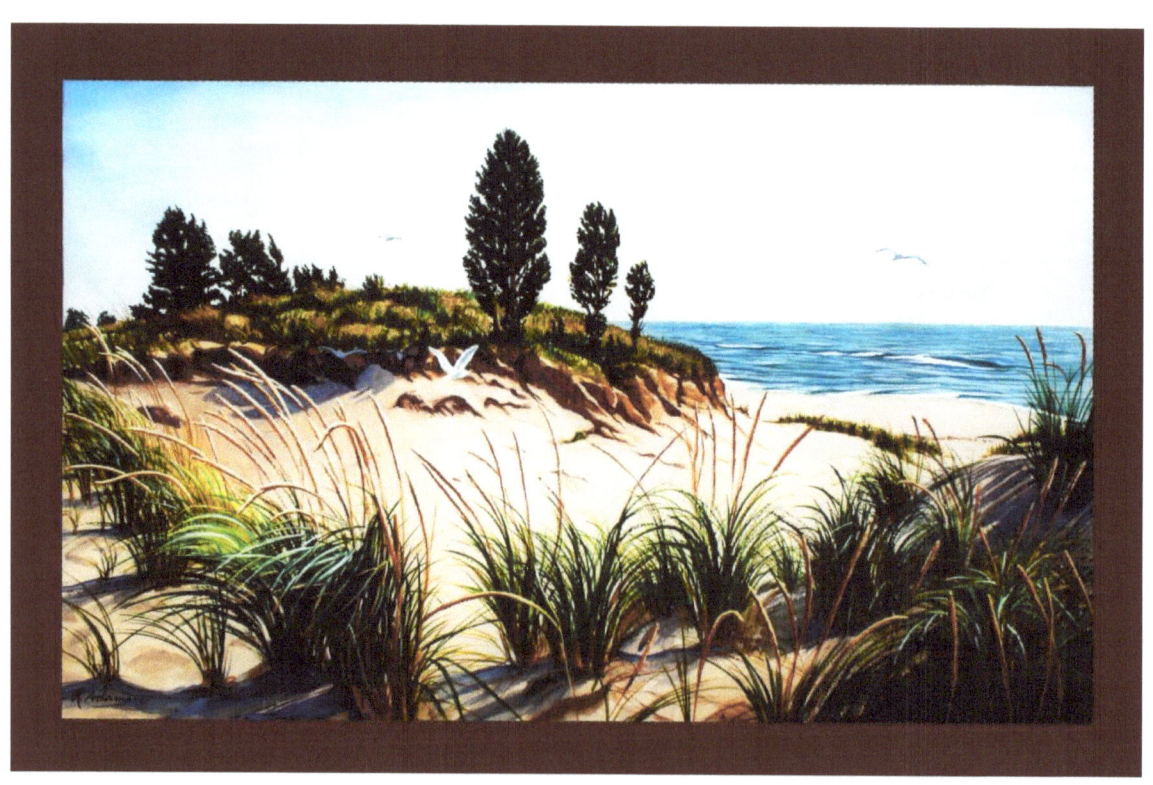

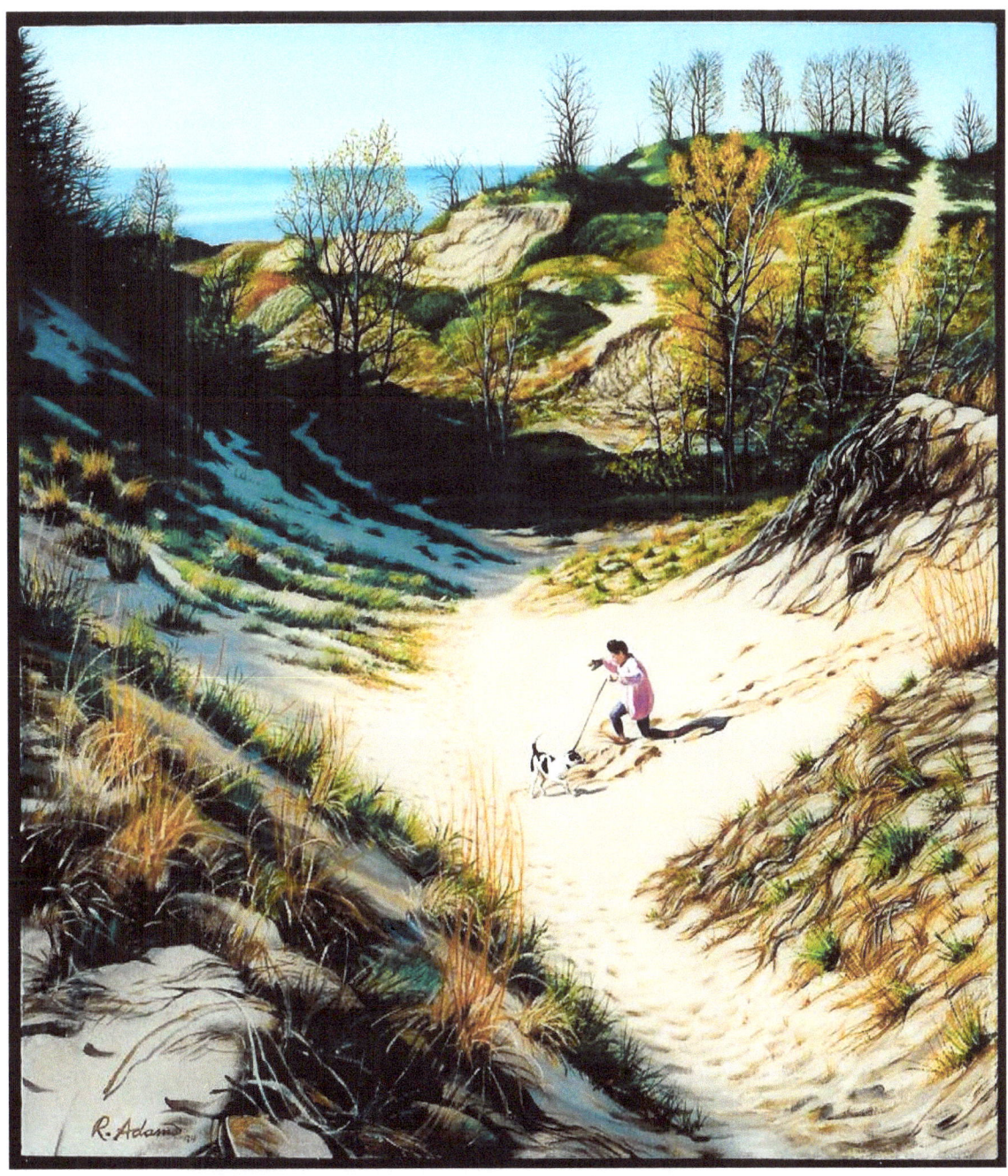

"Playfulness in the Sand Dunes"

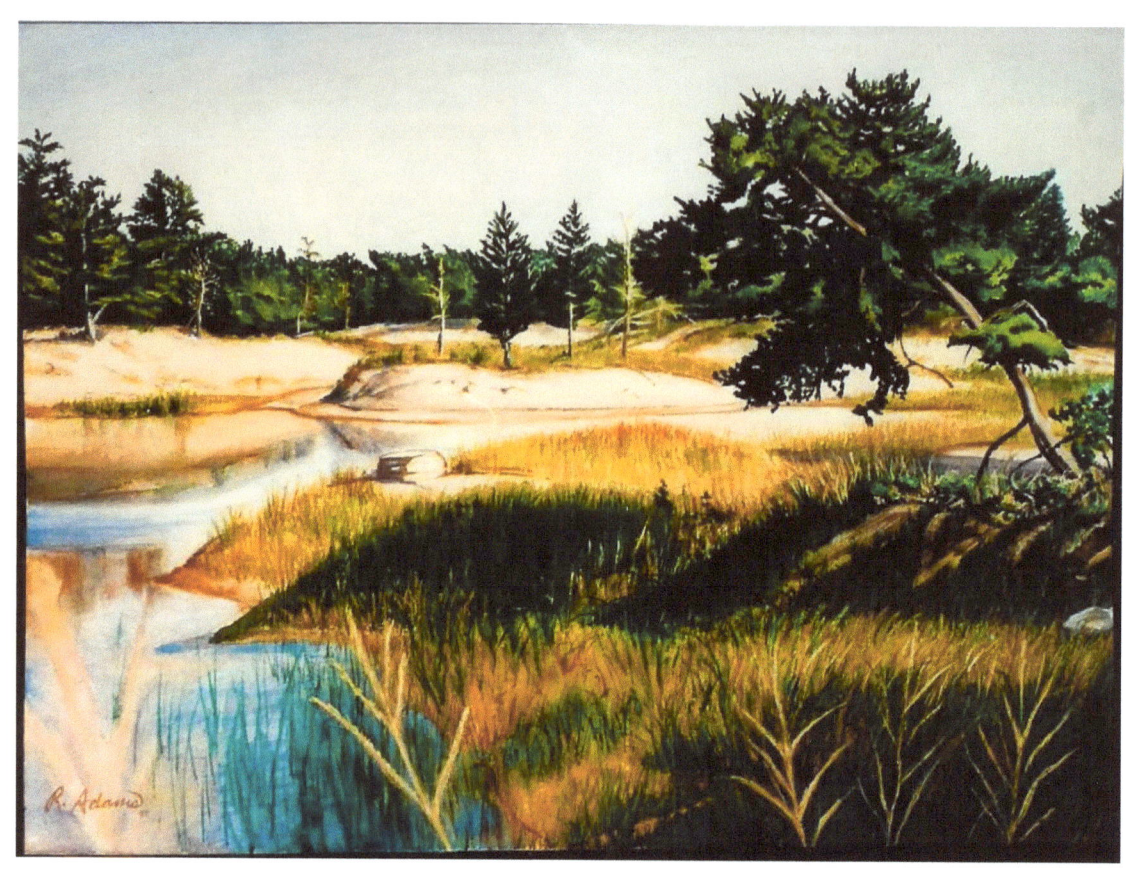

"Meditation"

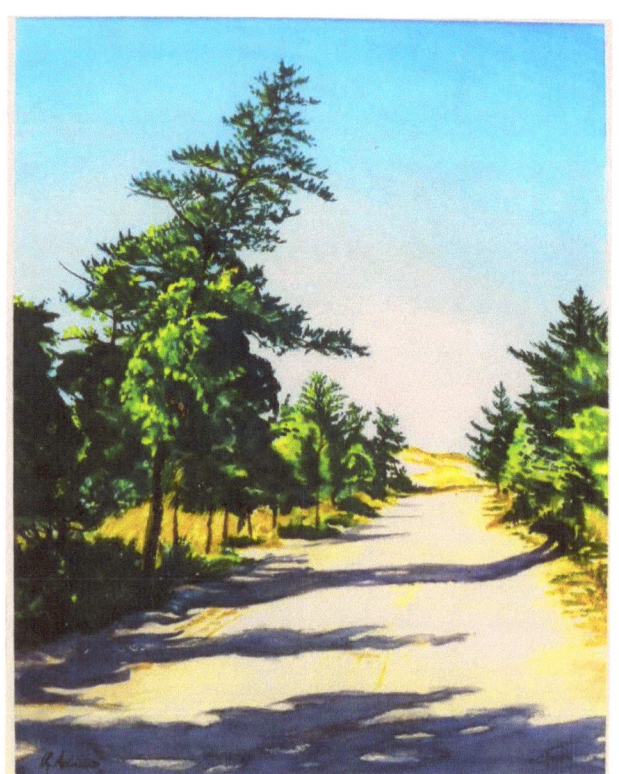

"End of Road"

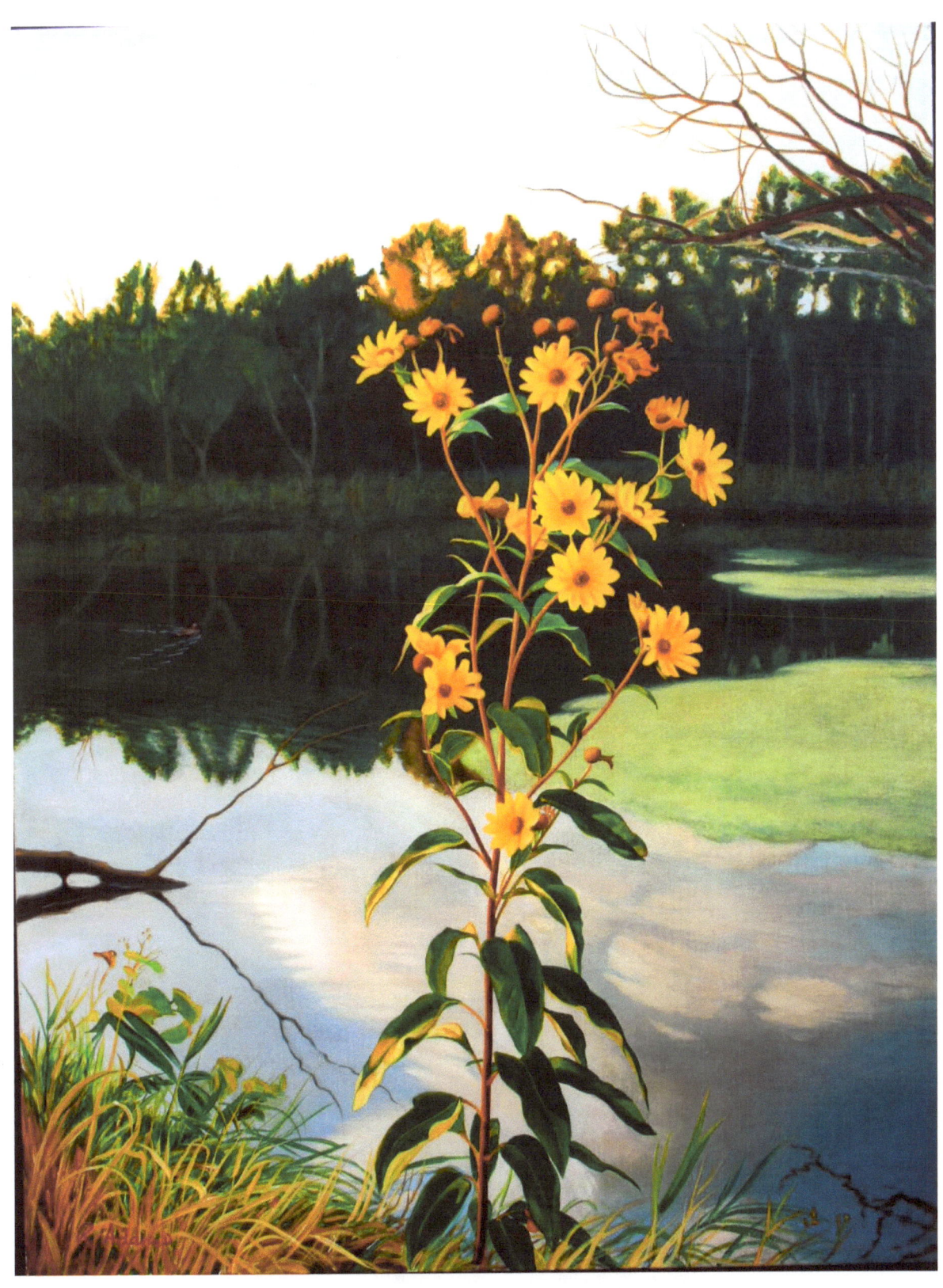

"Wild Sunflower"   (Many within the one.)

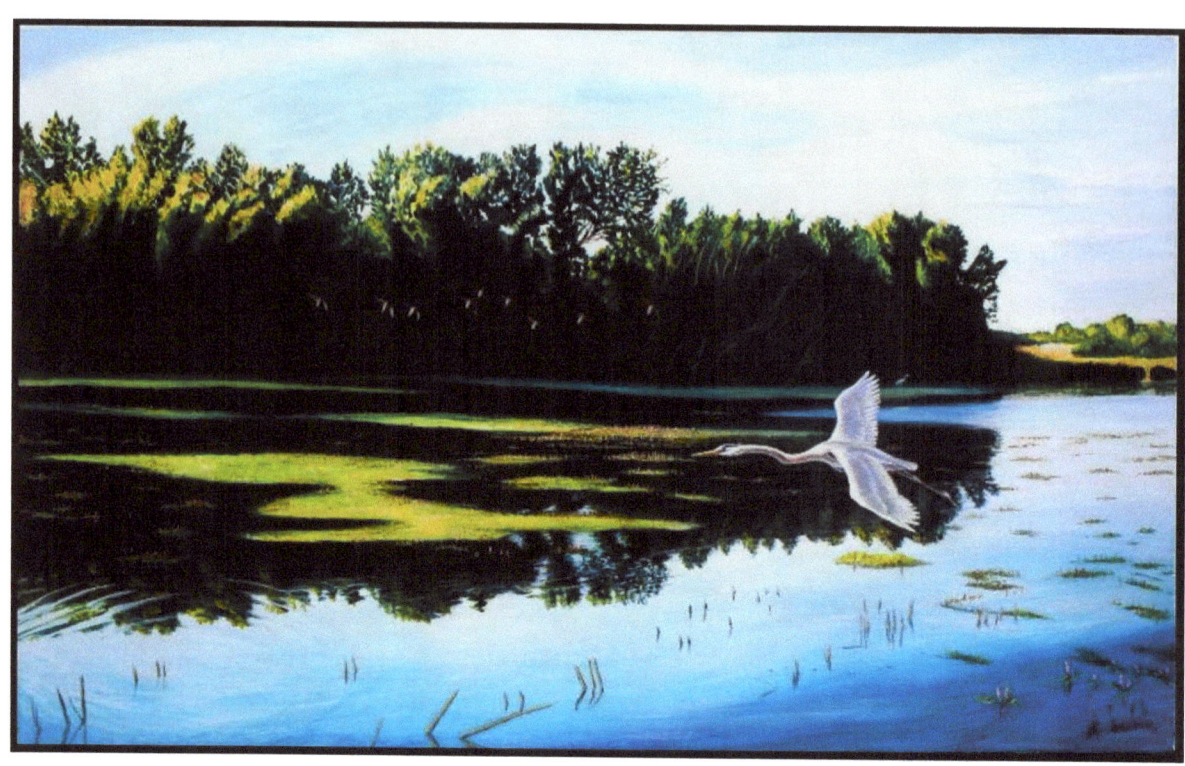

"The Wetlands"

"Going Home"

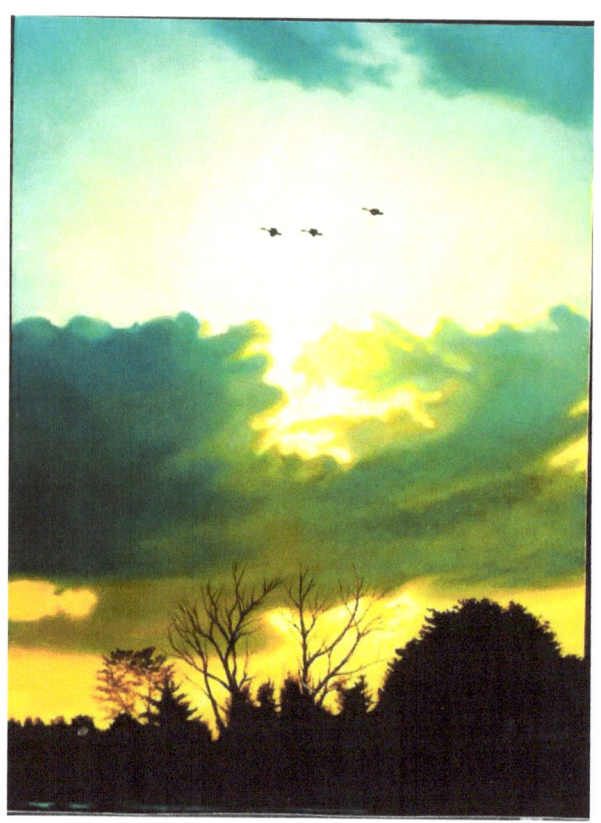

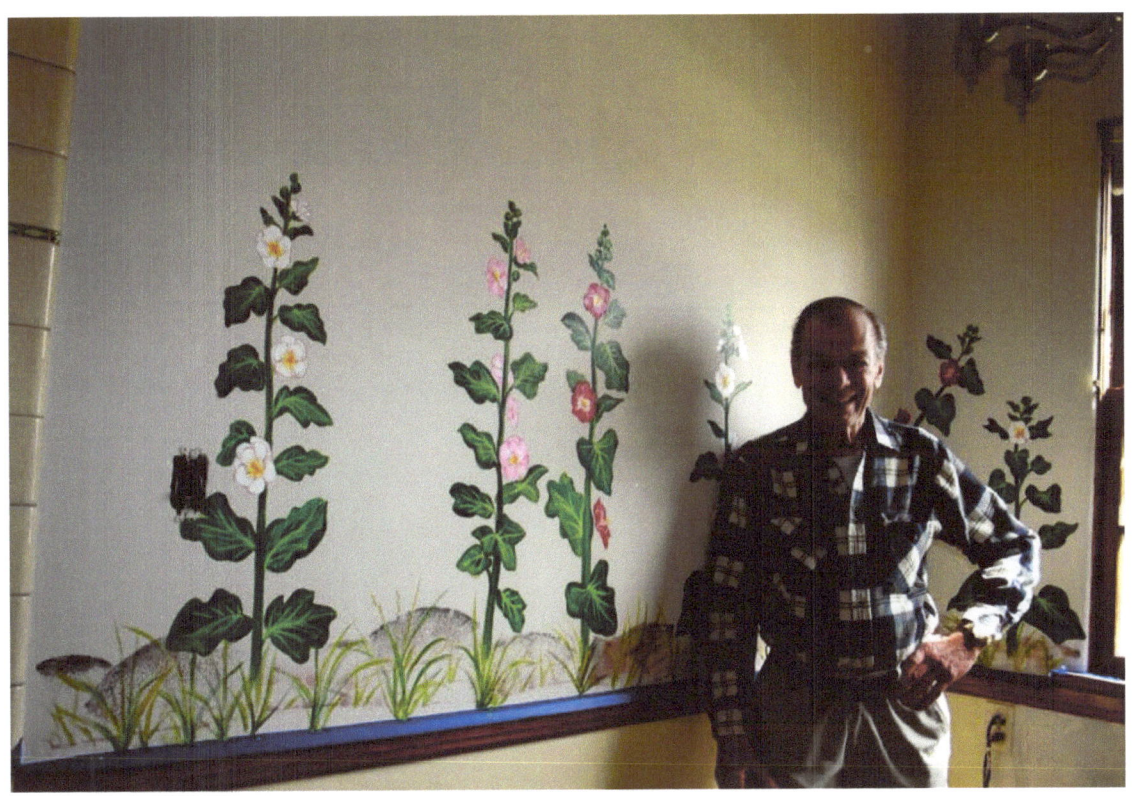

There was a time when I was called upon to paint some murals for various customers who wanted to decorate their walls instead of just painting them which was my usual work. In this particular case a Christian minister had a dark and rather dingy kitchen nook that he wanted to brighten up with some flowers and so he called upon me to do the work. It took about five days and during that time we became friends. At the end he invited me, if I cared to, to attend a service at his church, which I did. It was pretty good, and informative on Christ's teaching on the subject of peace. Many of Jesus Christ's teaching are in content very similar to the teachings of Gautama Buddha, which leads some to think that during his early youth and adulthood that he may have come across Buddhism and studied from it. At any rate, and having no real hard evidence of it one can only think that it is a possibility.

But this minister was very sincere, and had I not met the teacher much earlier I would perhaps be attending his church as I deeply respect both historical teachers.

The point is, that if you believe in God, God exists for you. Again, if you believe in Buddha, then the Buddha exists for you. It is not that God exists and therefore you believe in him, but rather it is because you believe in him that he exists. It is not that Buddha exists that you believe in him, it is rather that because you believe in him that he exists. Belief here means pure subjectivity. The basis of our religion is based upon our experience of it, not upon our intellectual and/or academic knowledge of it. If the truth does not come to us by way of the flesh it is not the truth, it belongs to doctrinal information as such. Our first experience with heat as hot teaches us about heat. Our first experience with cold is when we actually feel it, otherwise we really would only have knowledge about heat and cold by way of conceptualized knowledge. So it is particularly true when we seek into religion. When Reverend Akegarasu states that he gave up his adored God and Buddha in the high heavens that he preyed to to get power for himself, along with his Nembutsu, this is what he means.

27

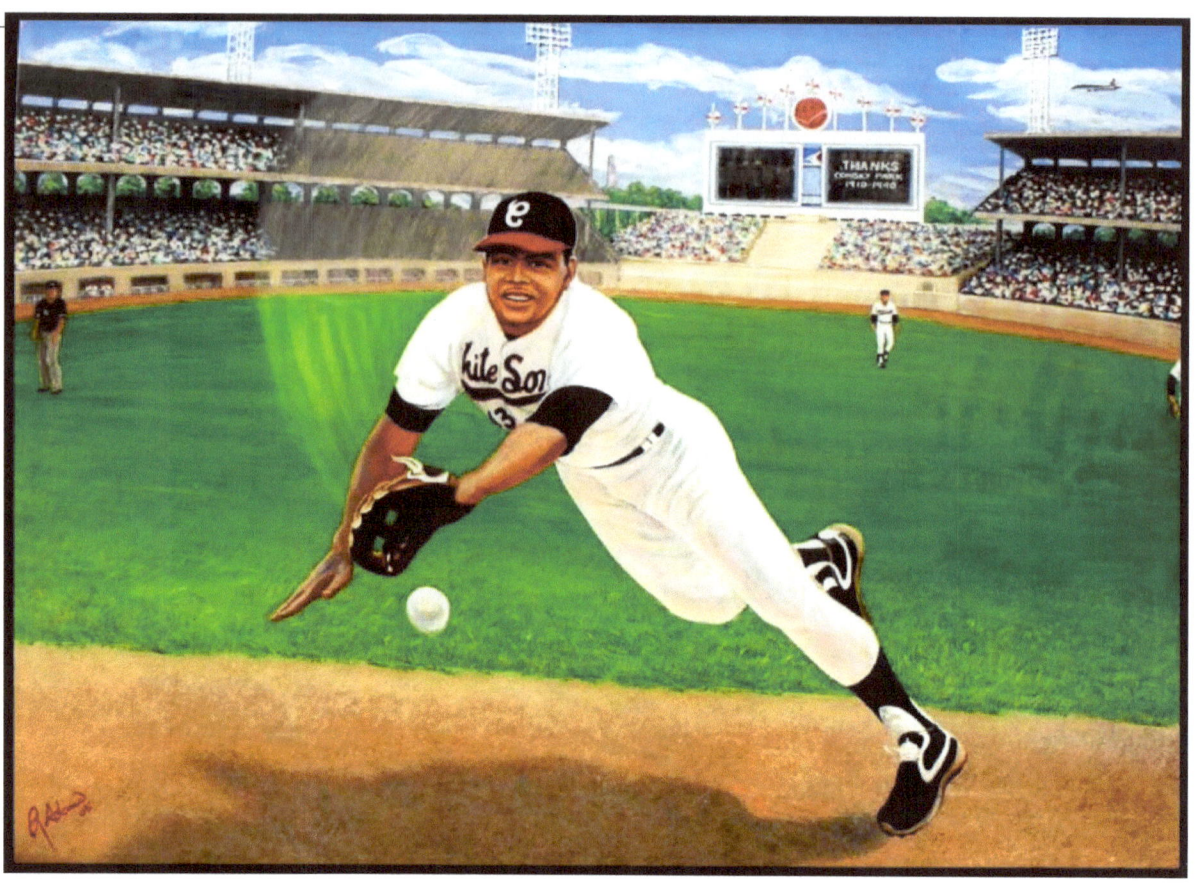

"Ozzie Guillen the Player" (a commissioned work)

"His Sweetness" " Walter Payton" (a commissioned work)

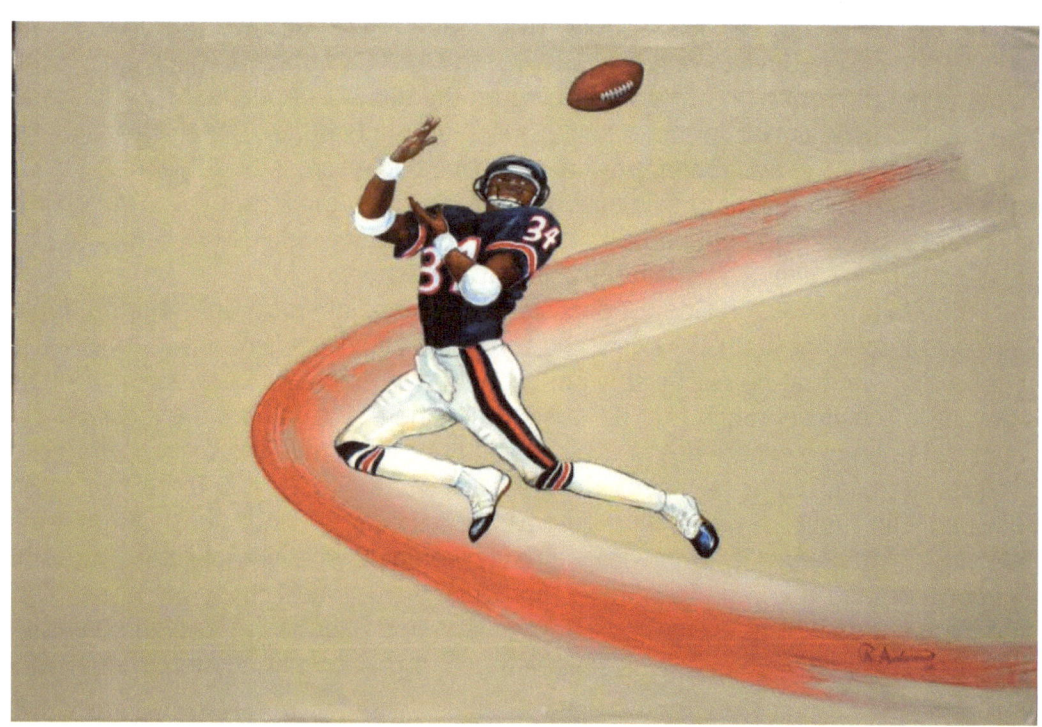

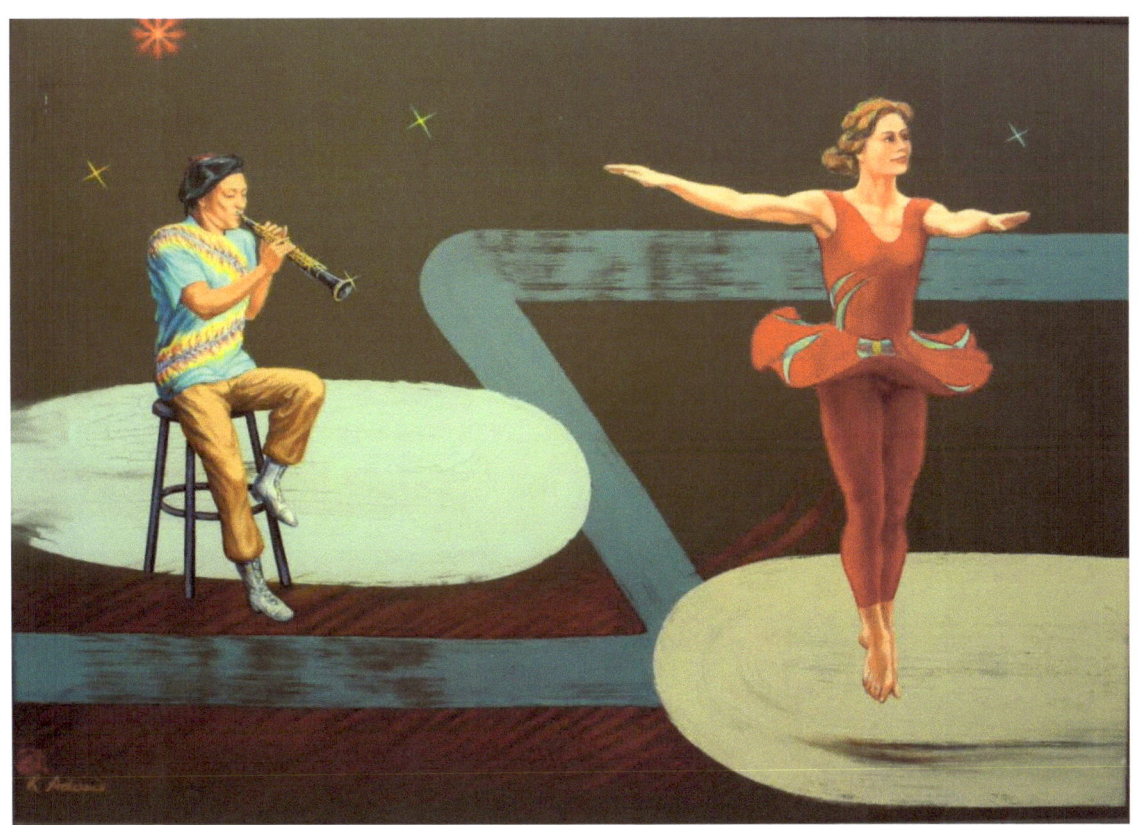

"Jazz Dancer"

"Greetings!"

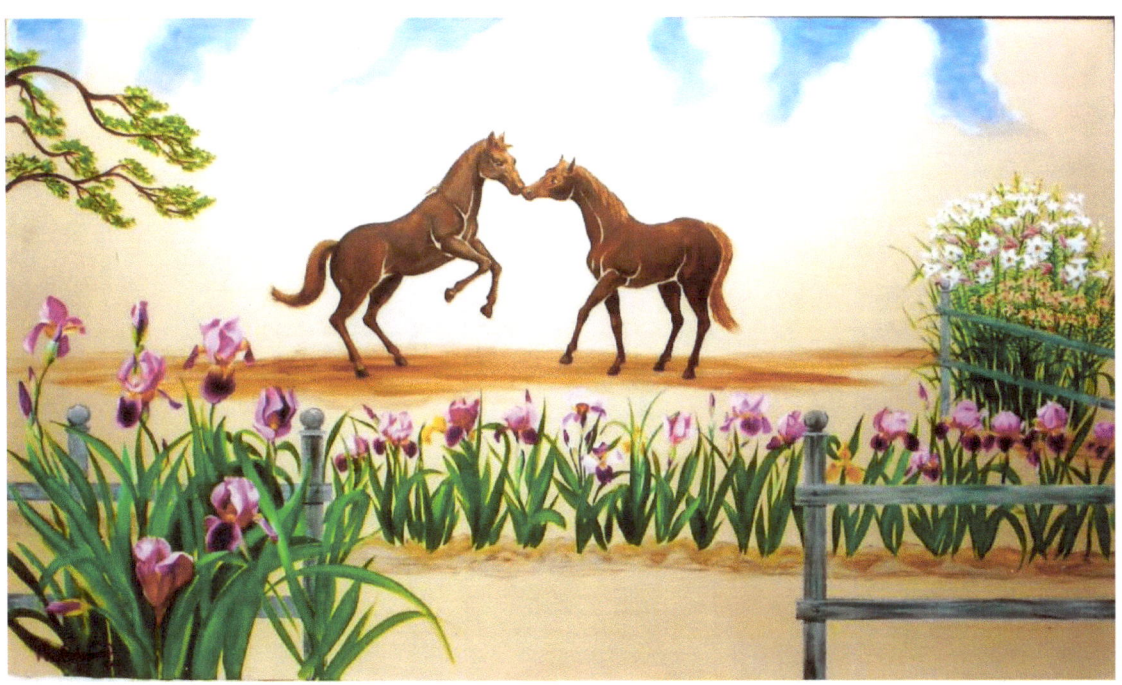

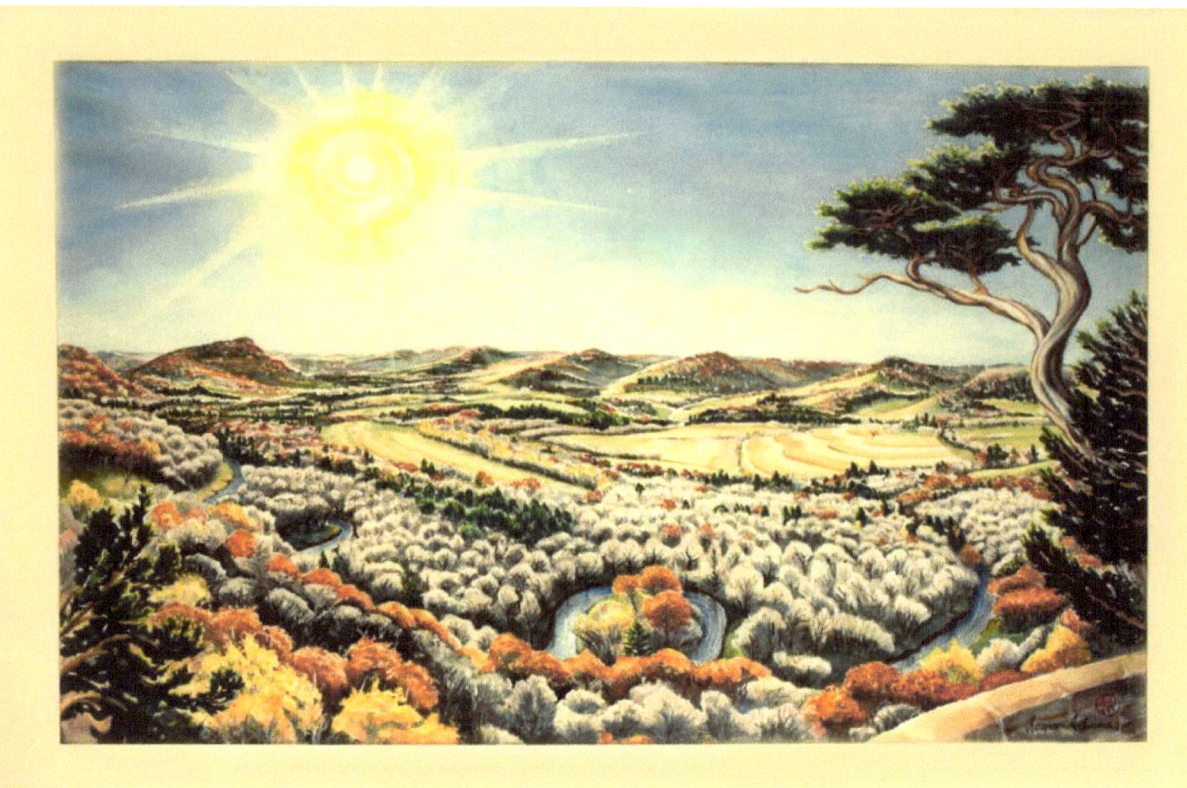

"God's Country"   (Northwestern Wisconsin)

"Cow Country"   (Northwestern Wisconsin)

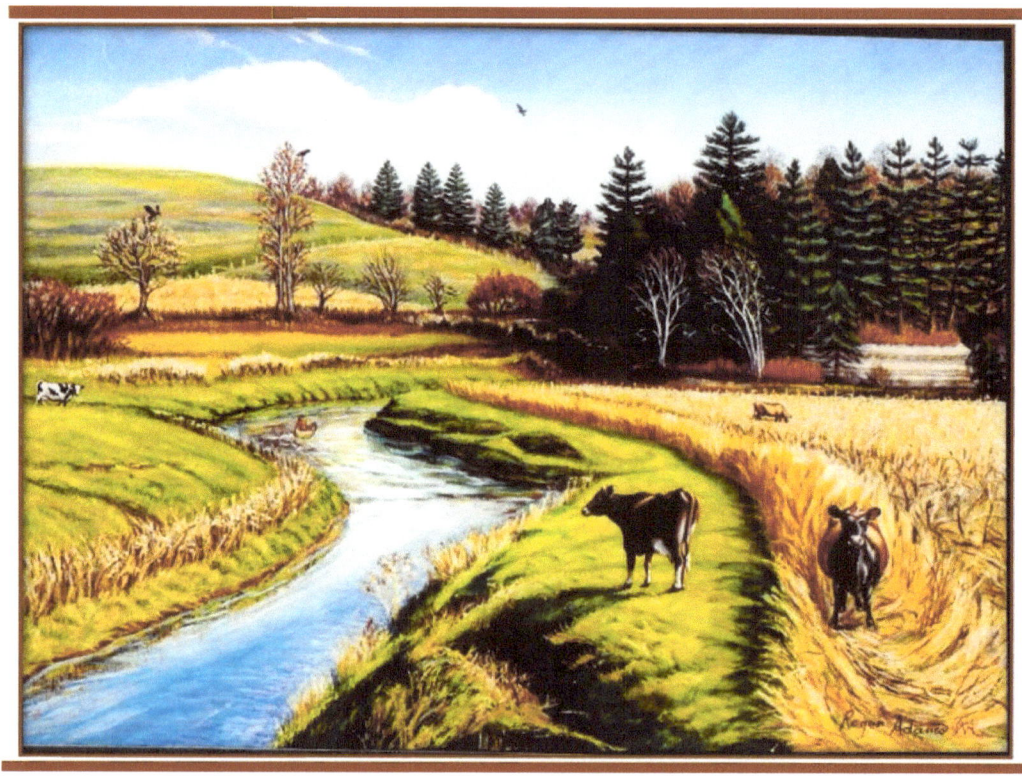

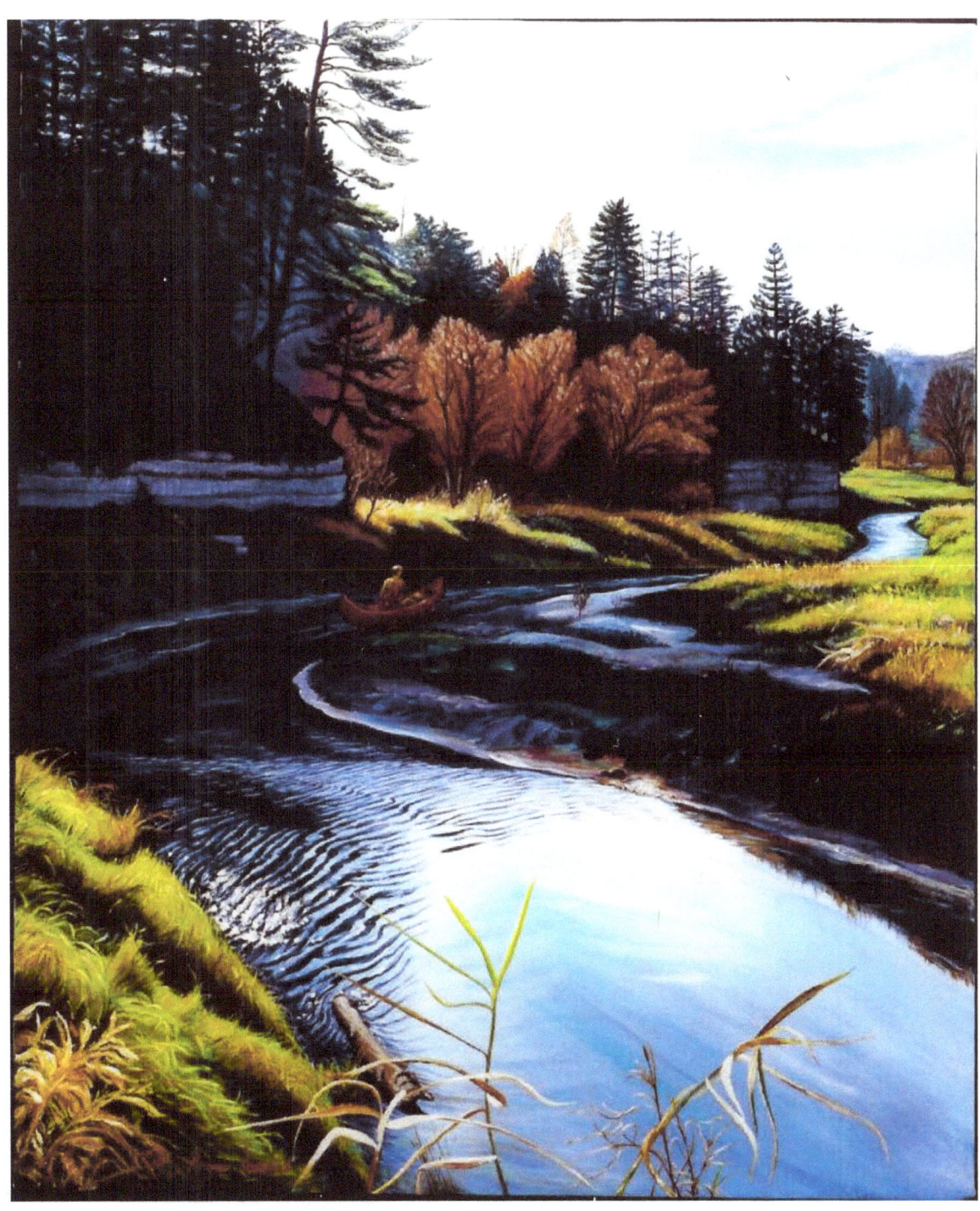

"Canoe Trip Down the Pistakee River" (Northwestern Wisconsin)

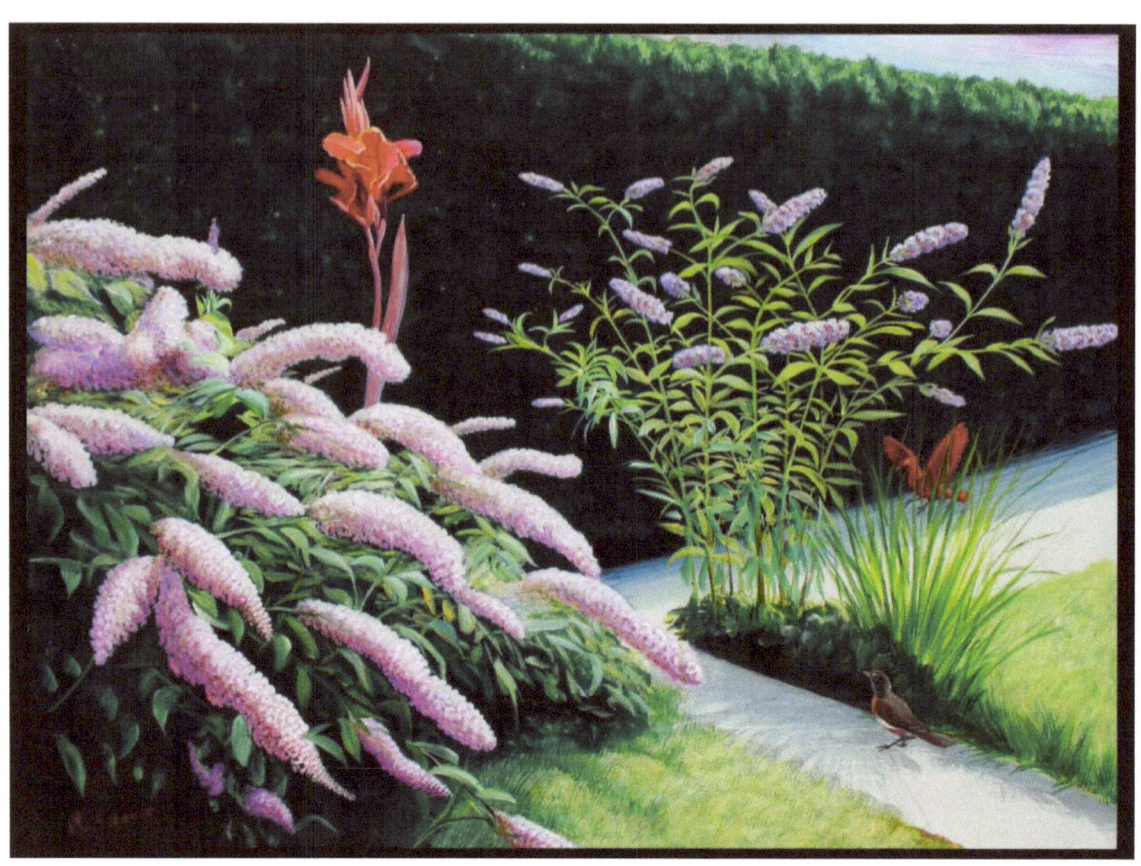

"Butterfly Bush"

"Orange Blossom Bush"

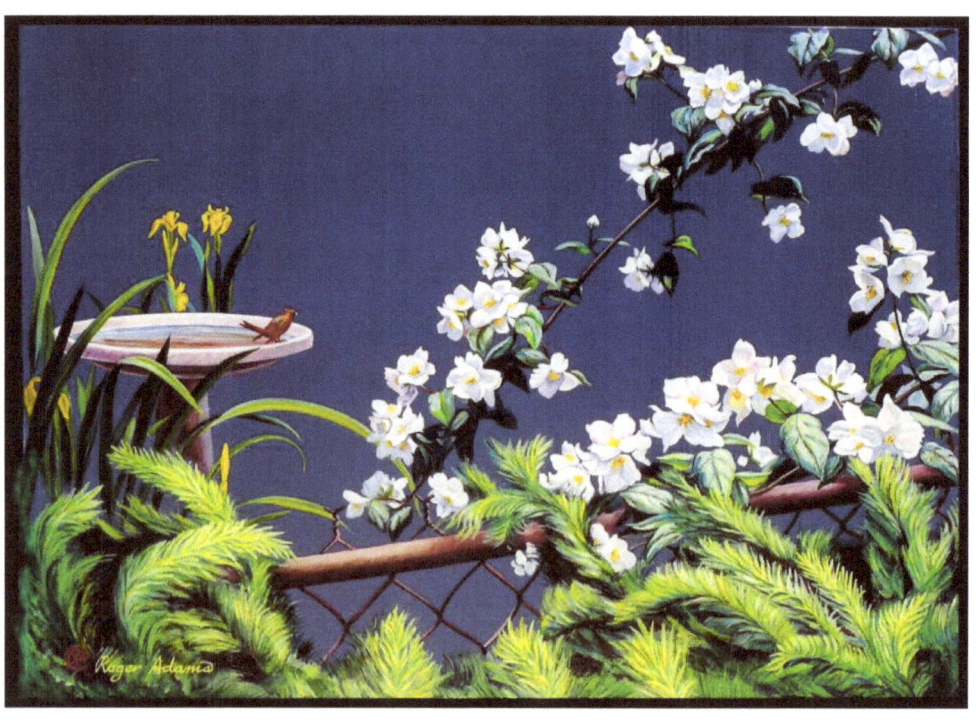

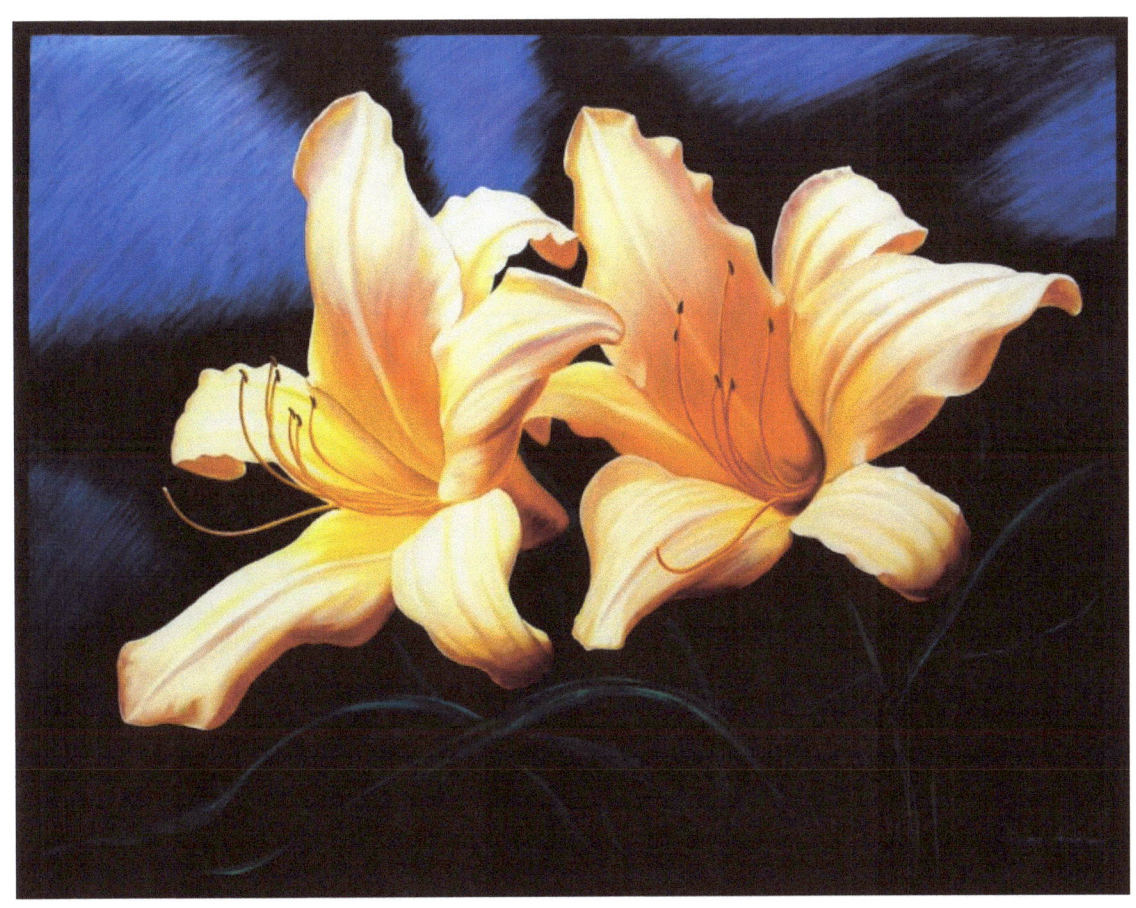

"Duet"

"The Apiarist"

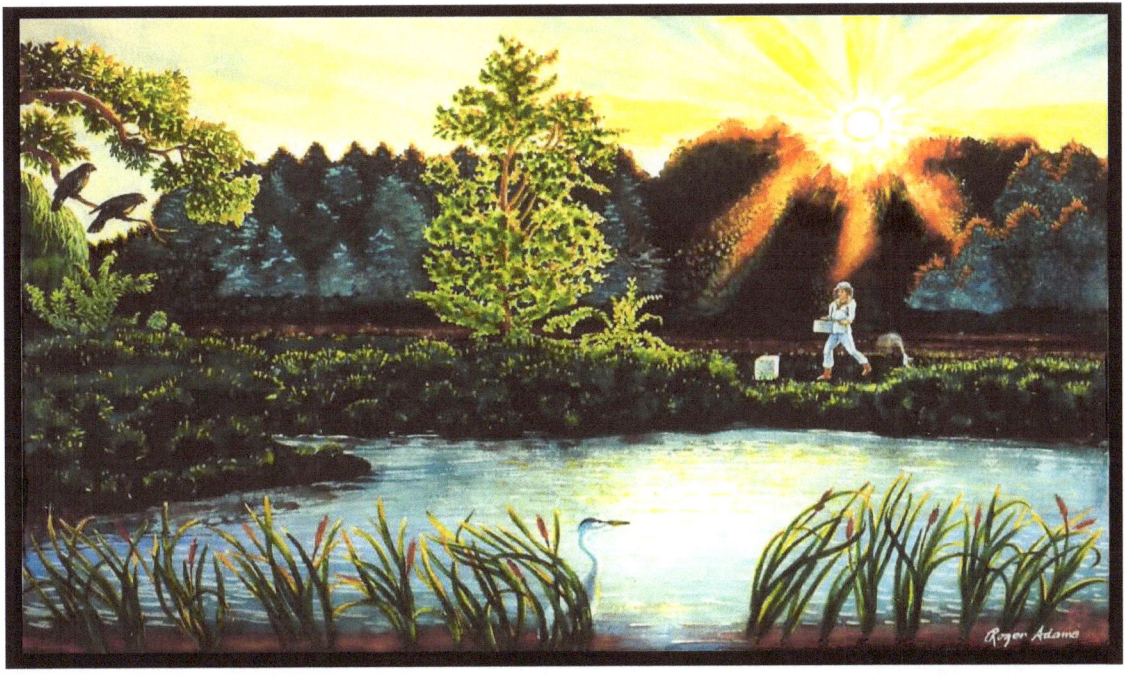

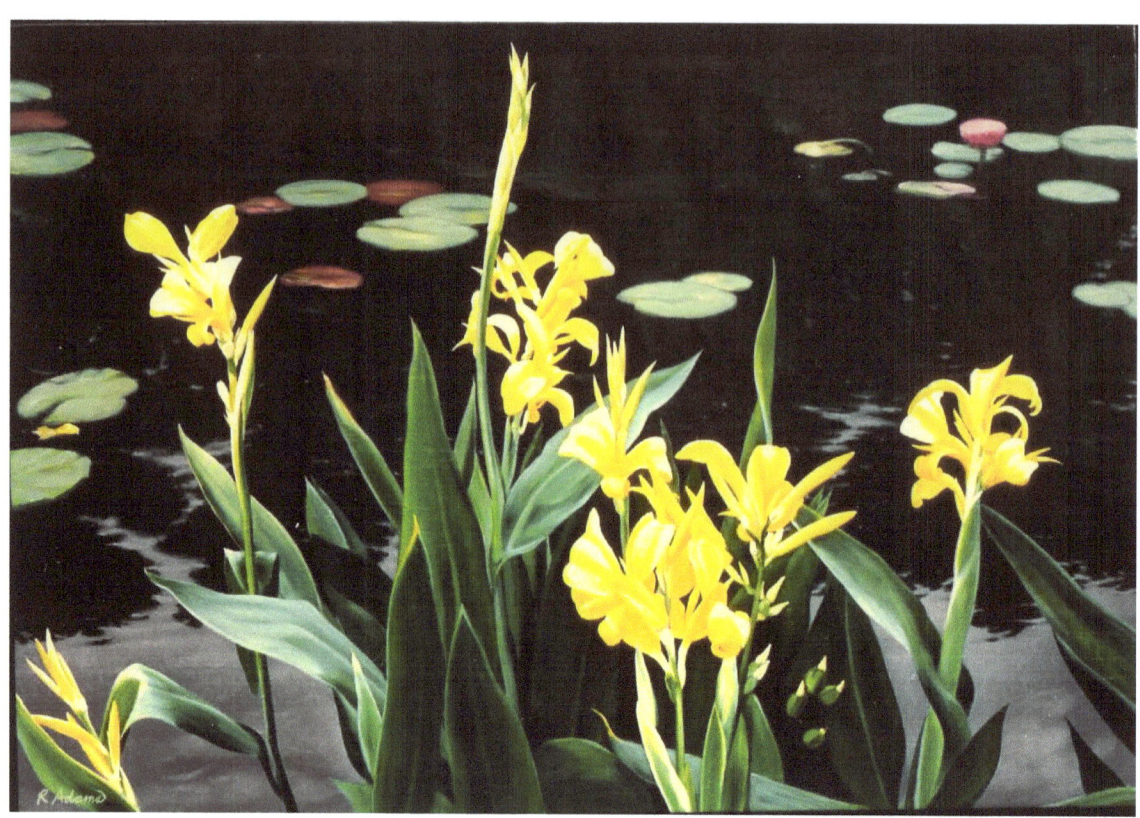

"Lilies by the Pond"

"Evening Pond"

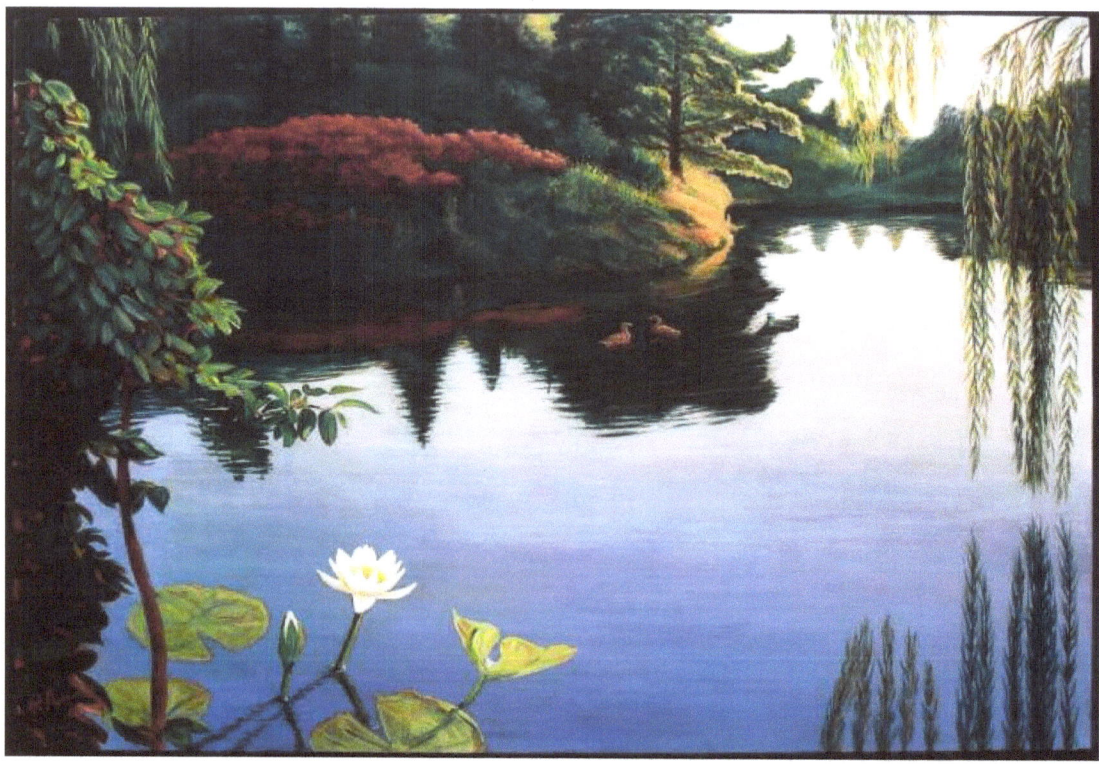

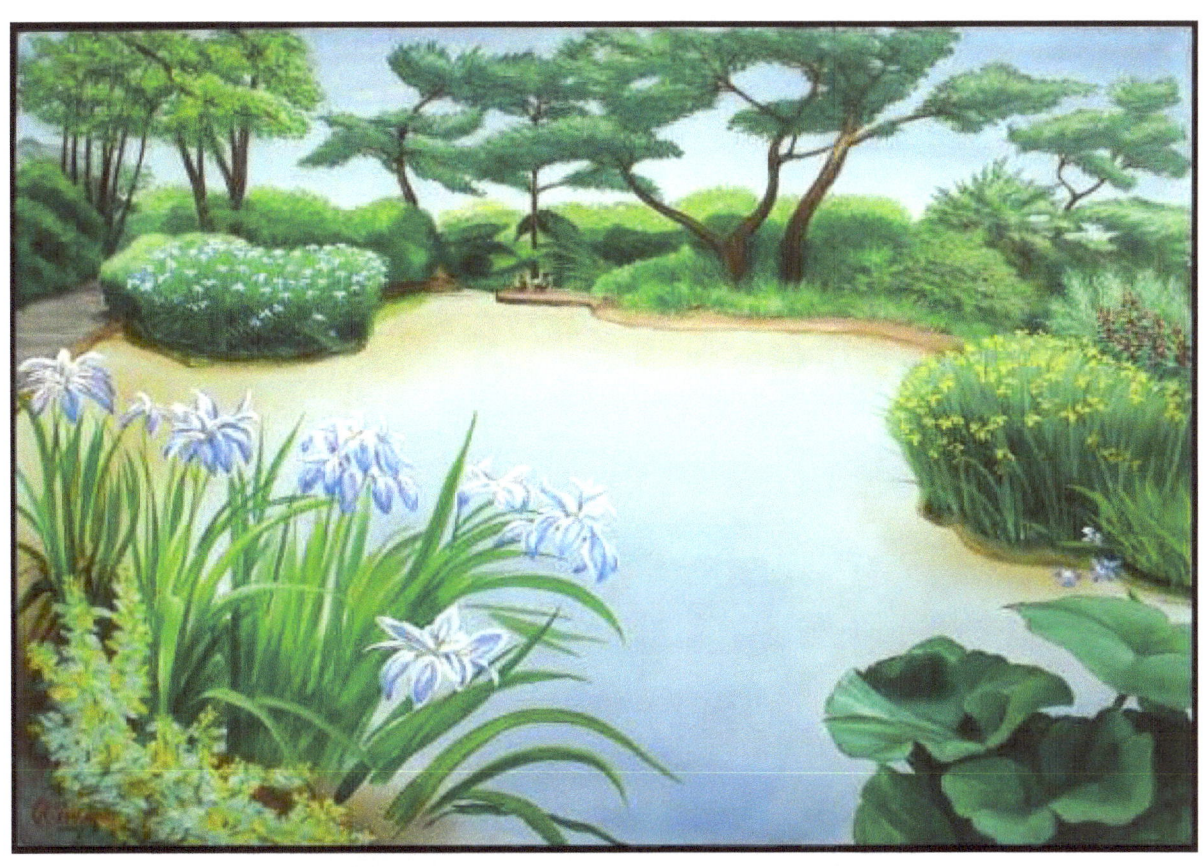

"Dancing Trees"

"Red Lilies"

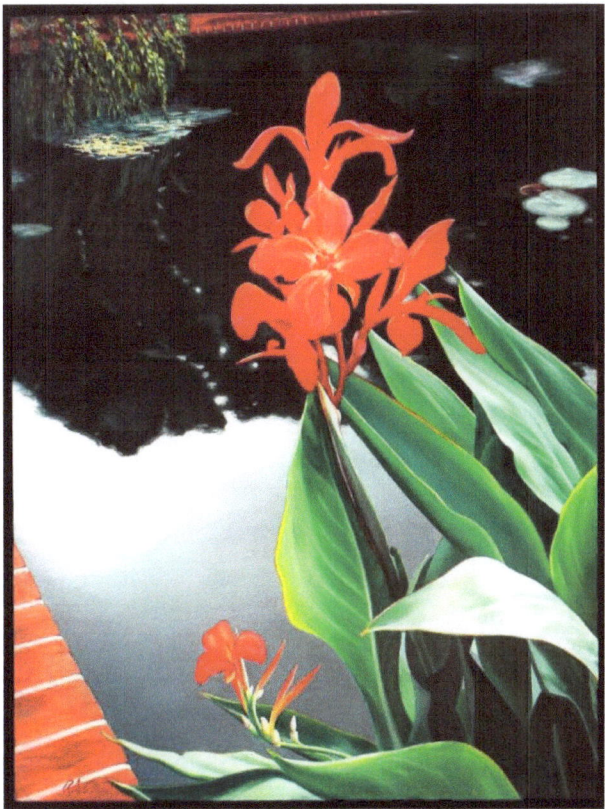

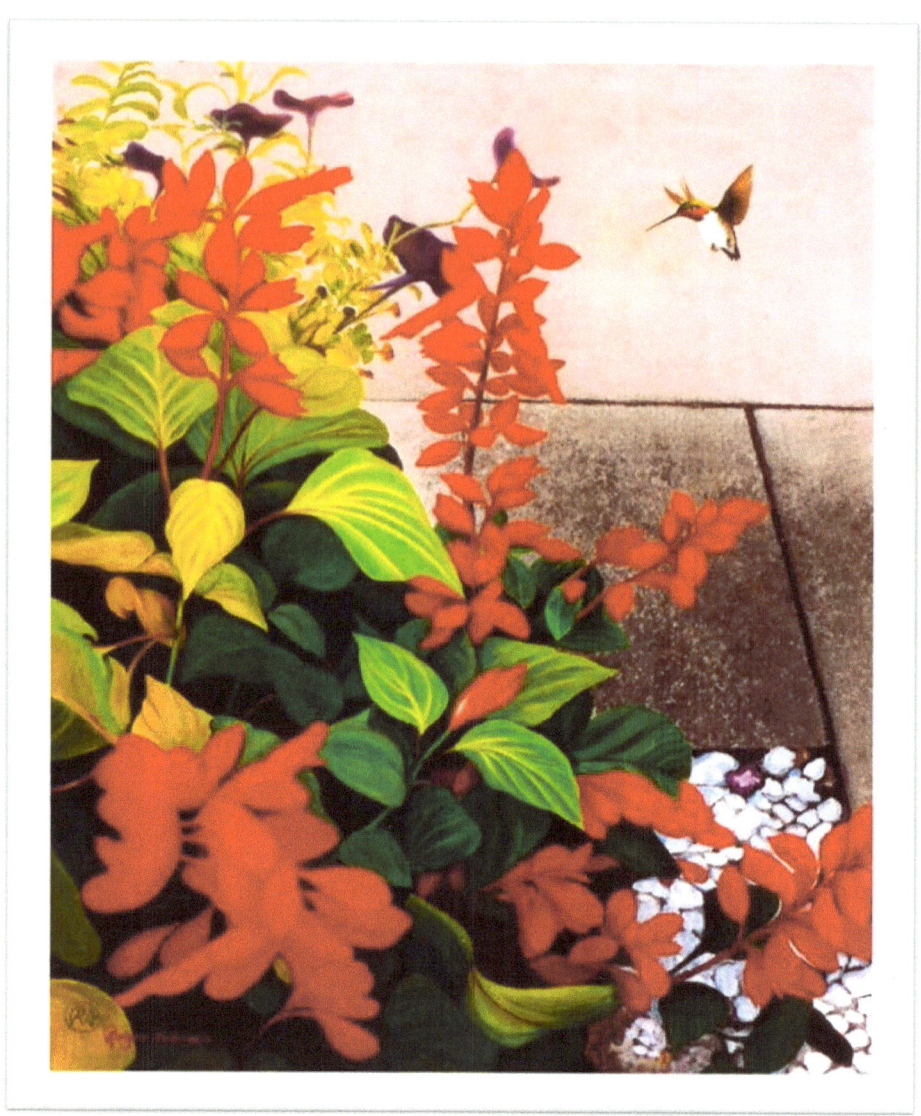

"Ruby-throated Hummingbird"

"Dancing Salsa"

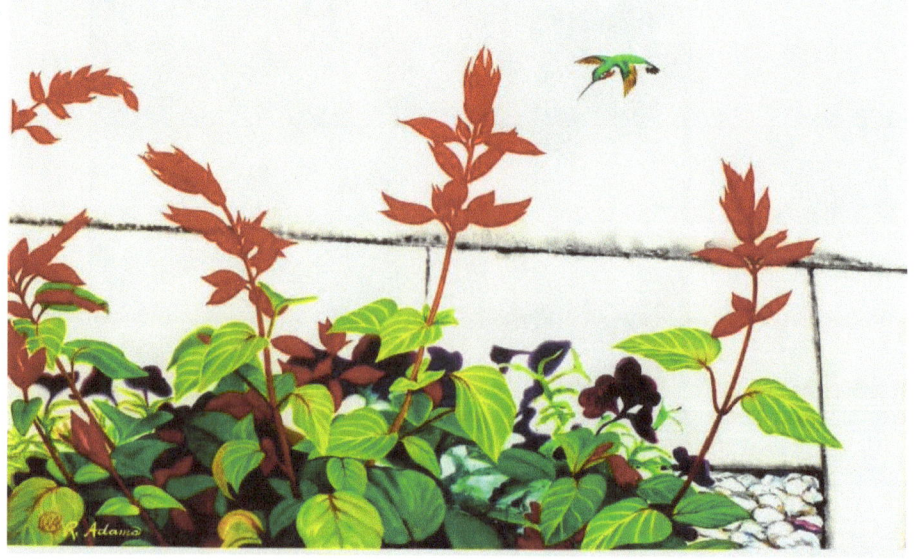

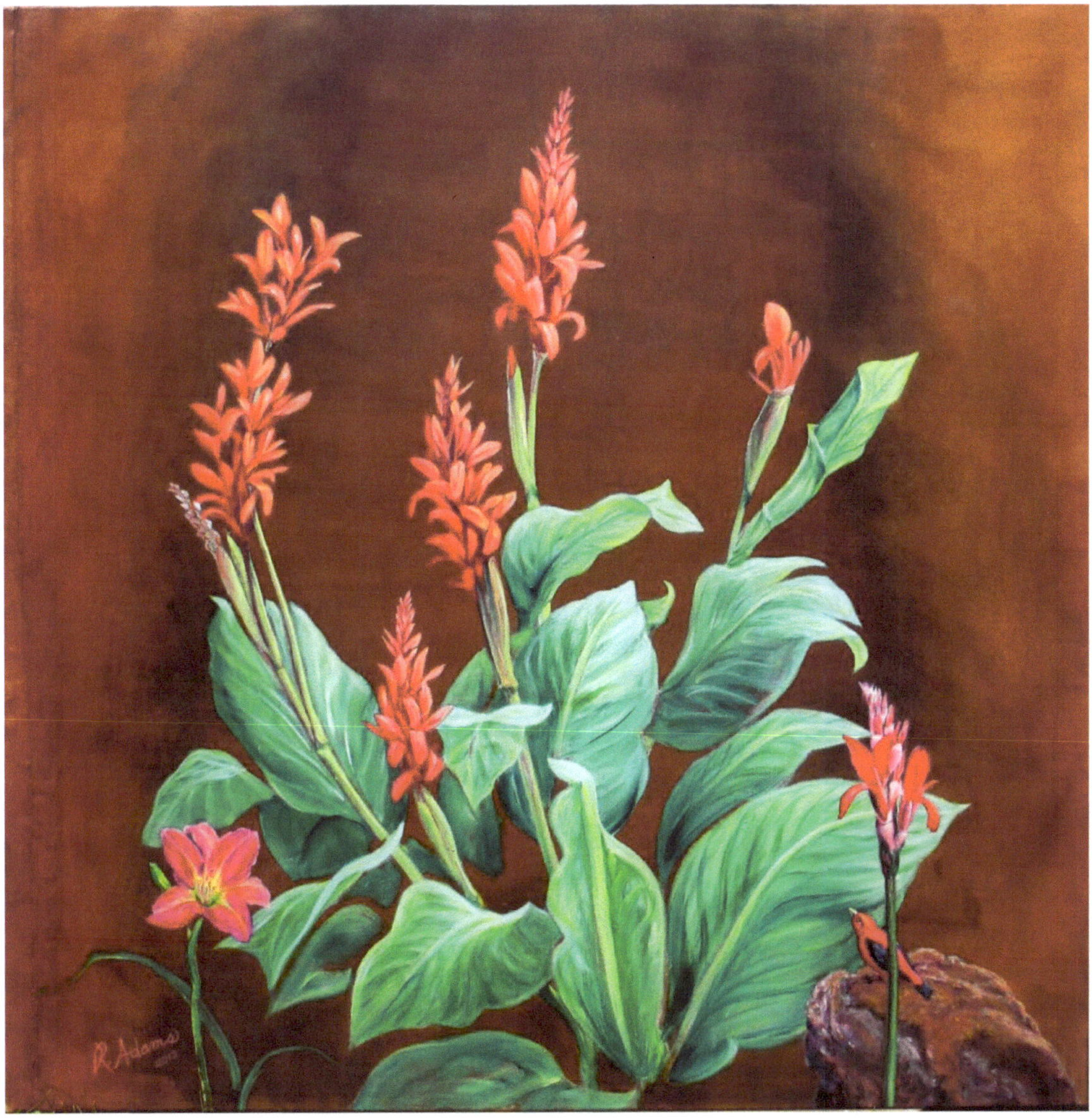

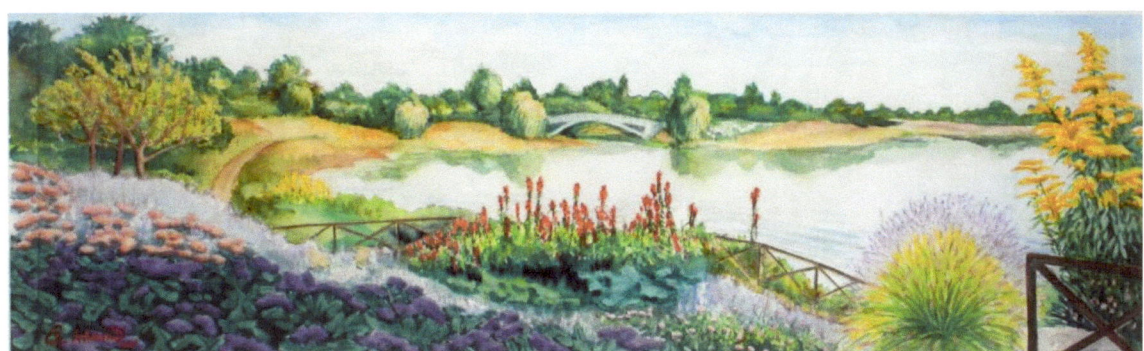

"Cana Lilly"

"Botanic Garden"

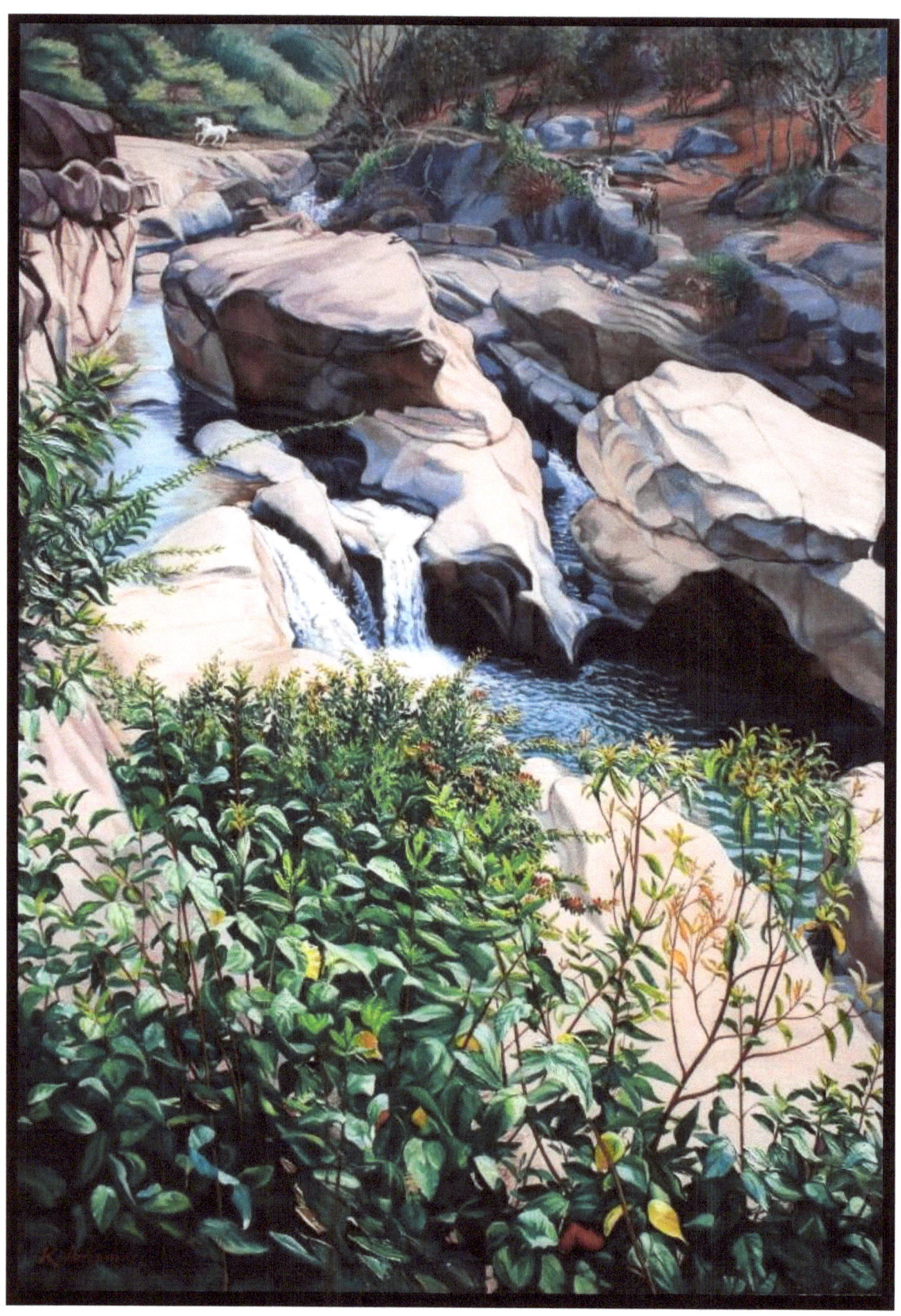

"Life Among the Rocks" (Mexico)

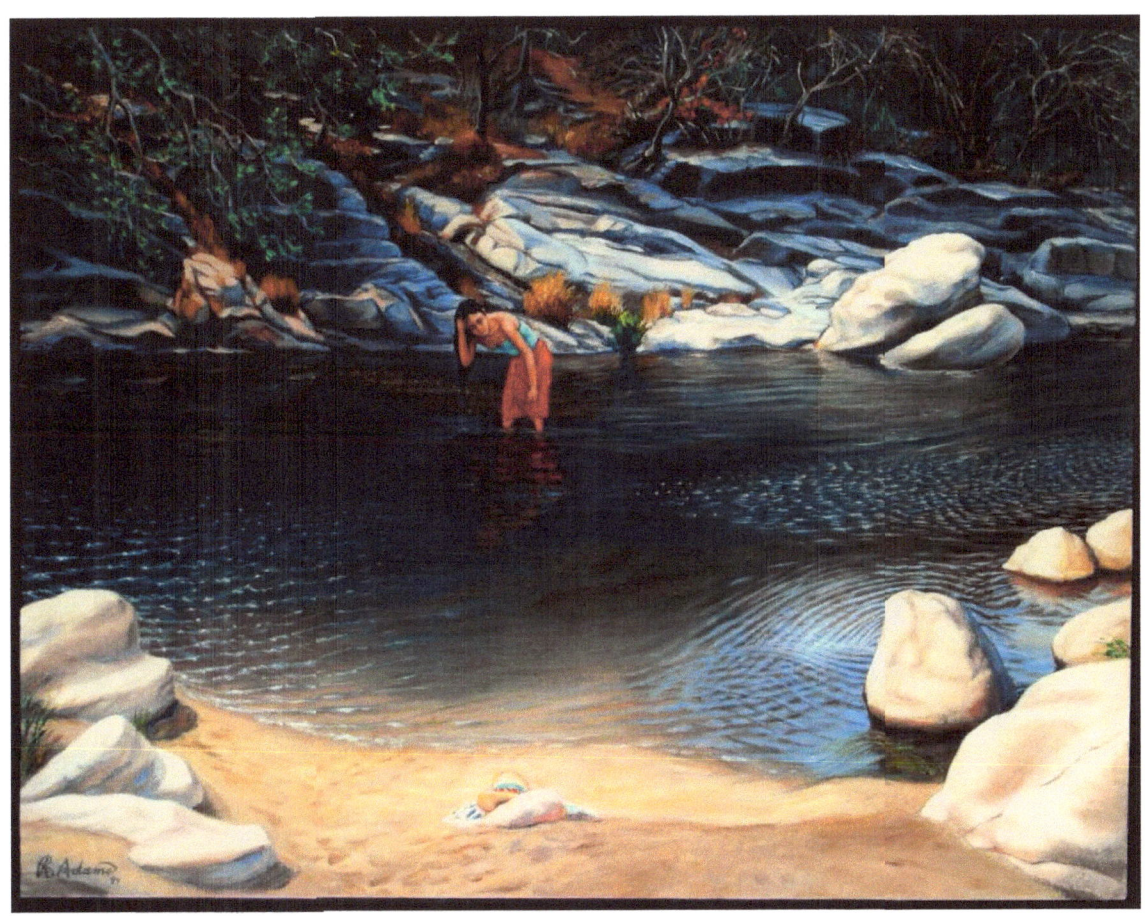

"Afternoon Respite" (Mexico)

"Gulls"

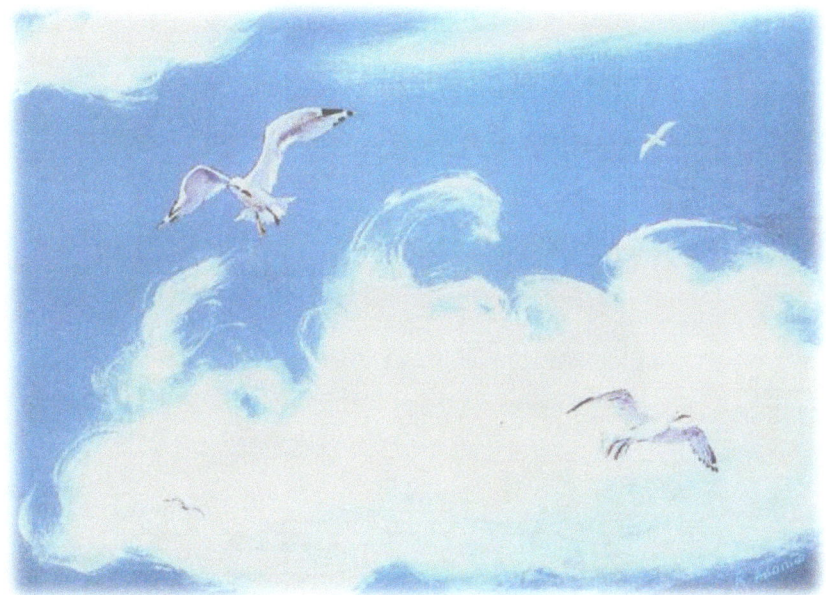

(Ceiling mural for a baby's room.)

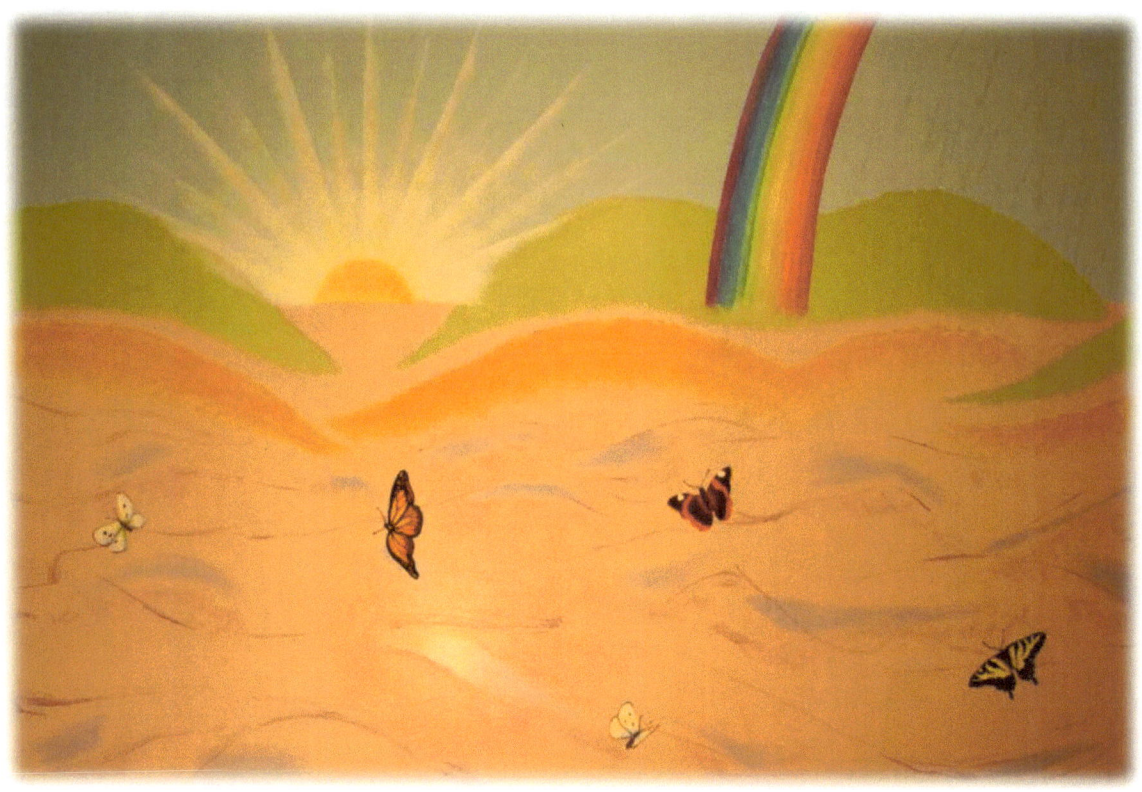

(Butterfly mural design for a girl's playroom.)

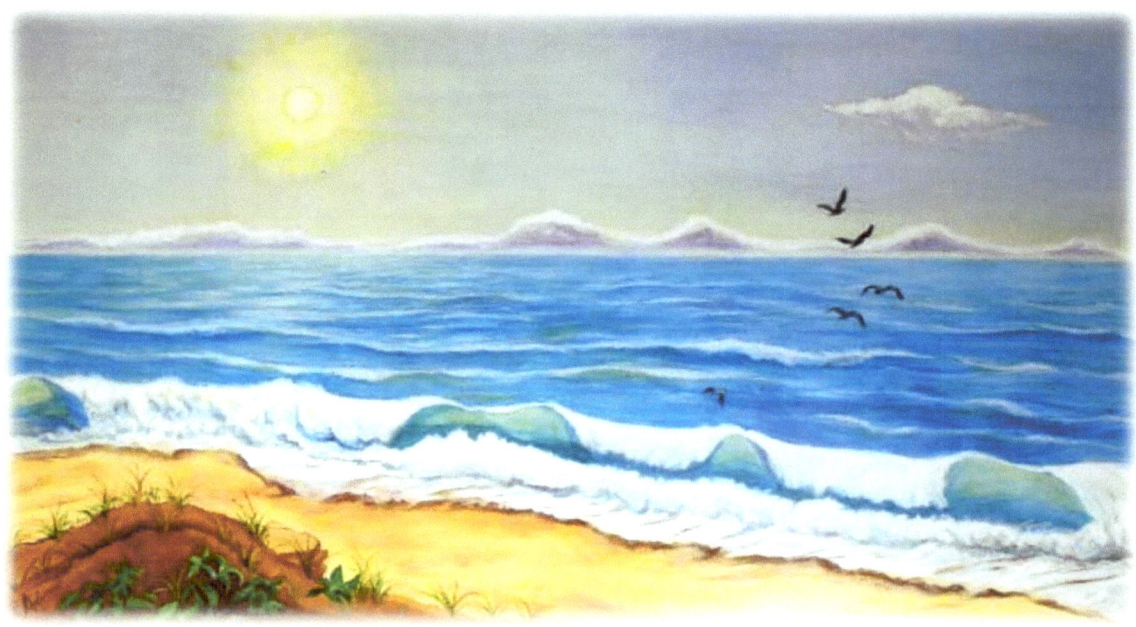

(Mural design for "man's room.")

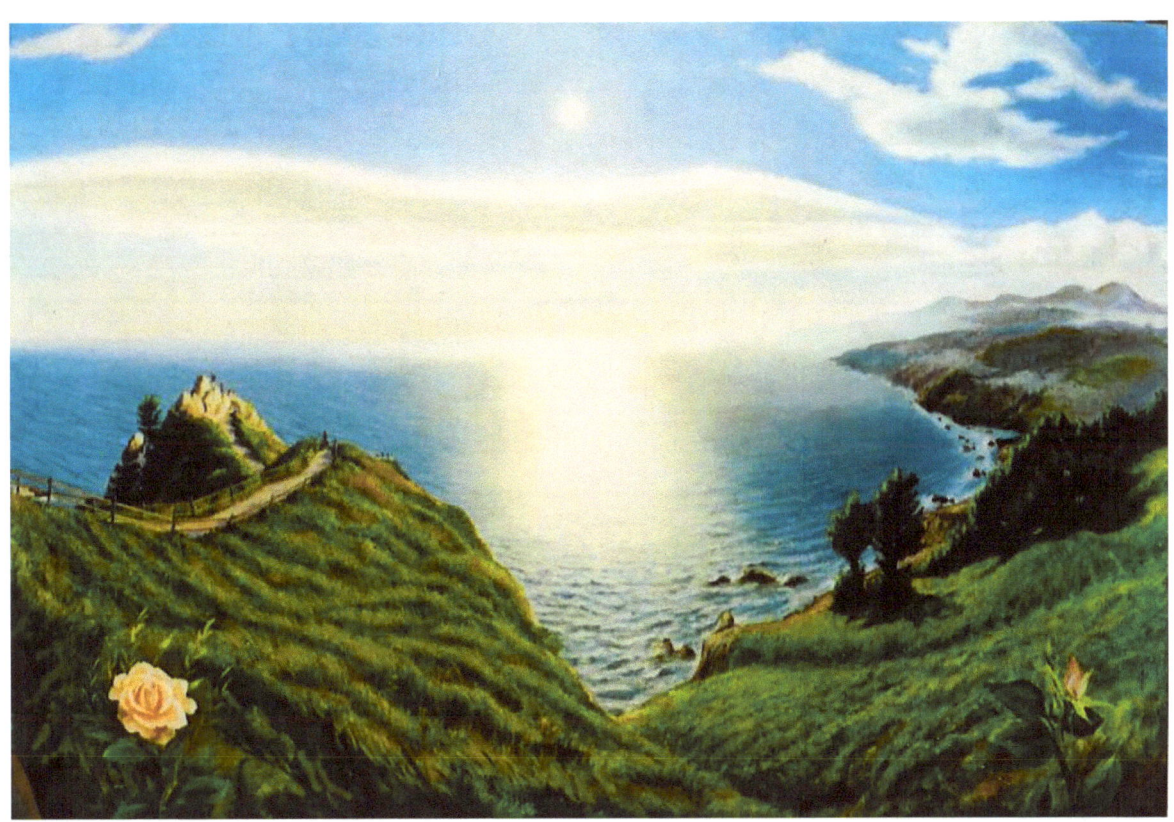

"Pacific View"

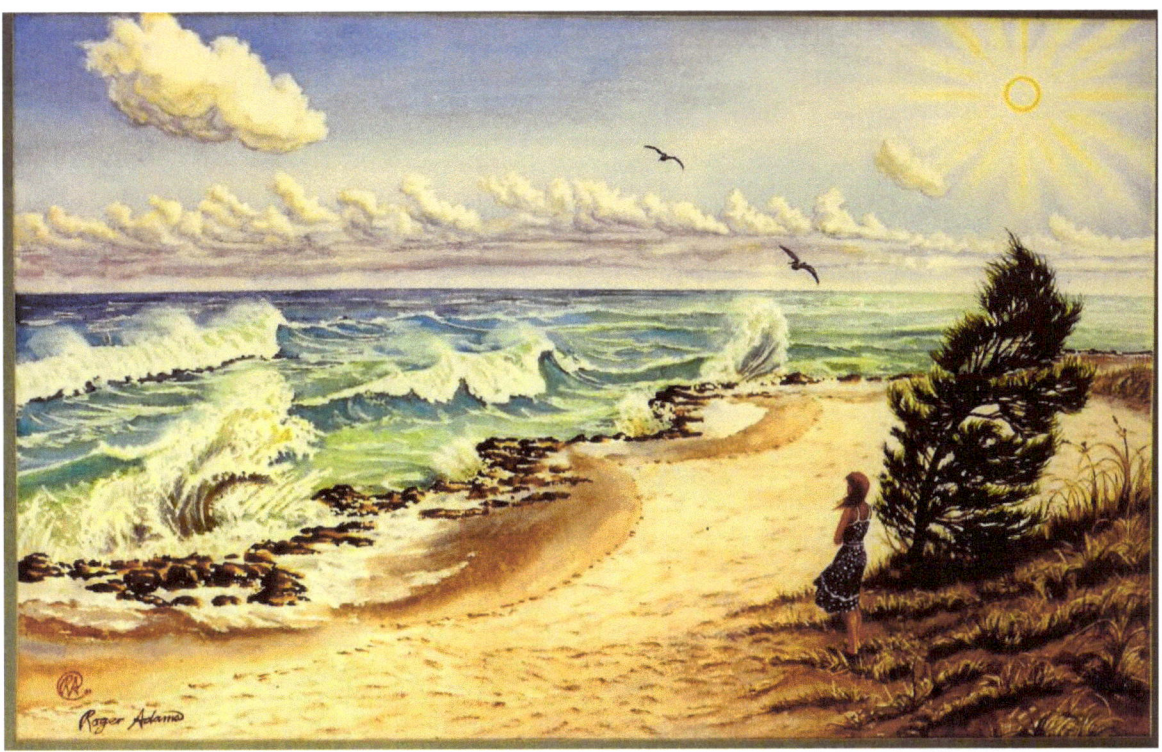

"Turbulent Ocean"

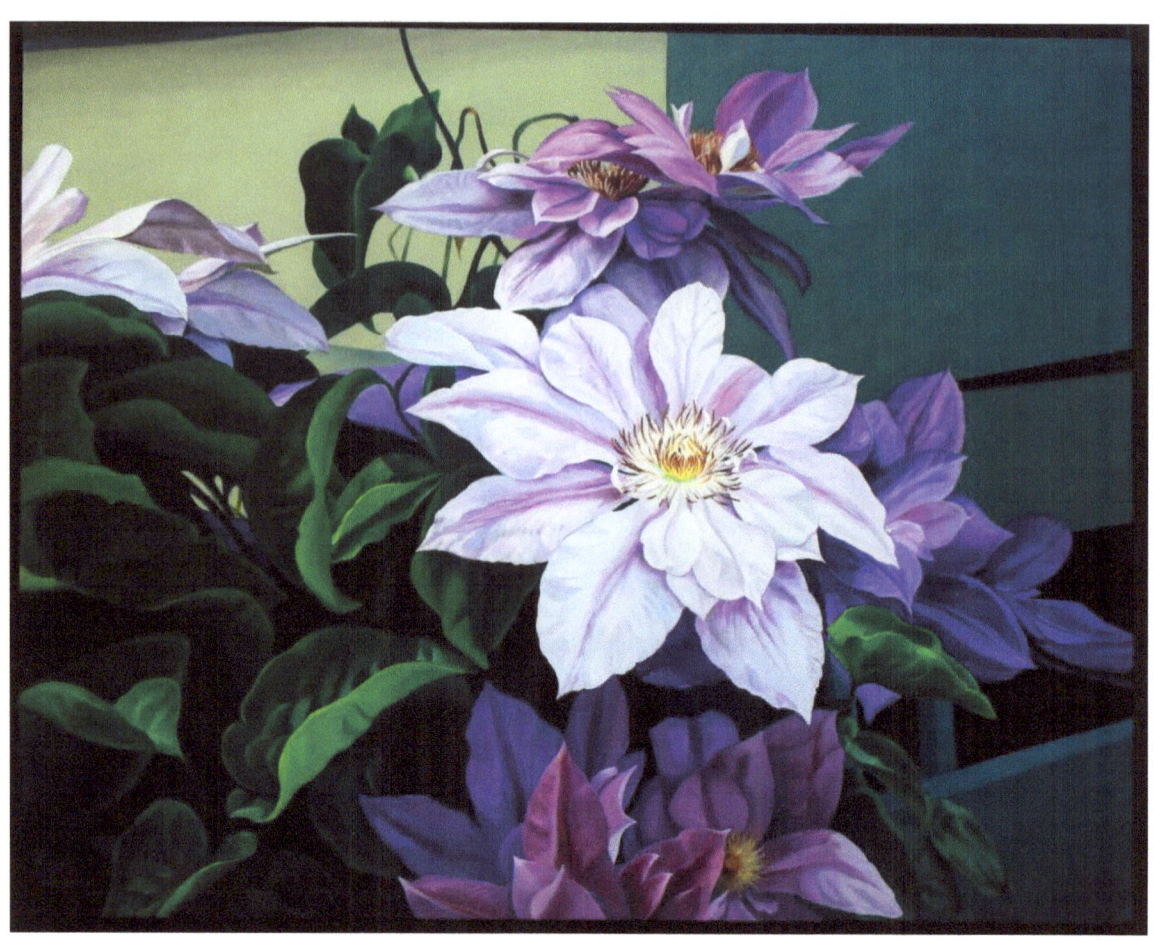

"Bright Star"

"Moon Glow"

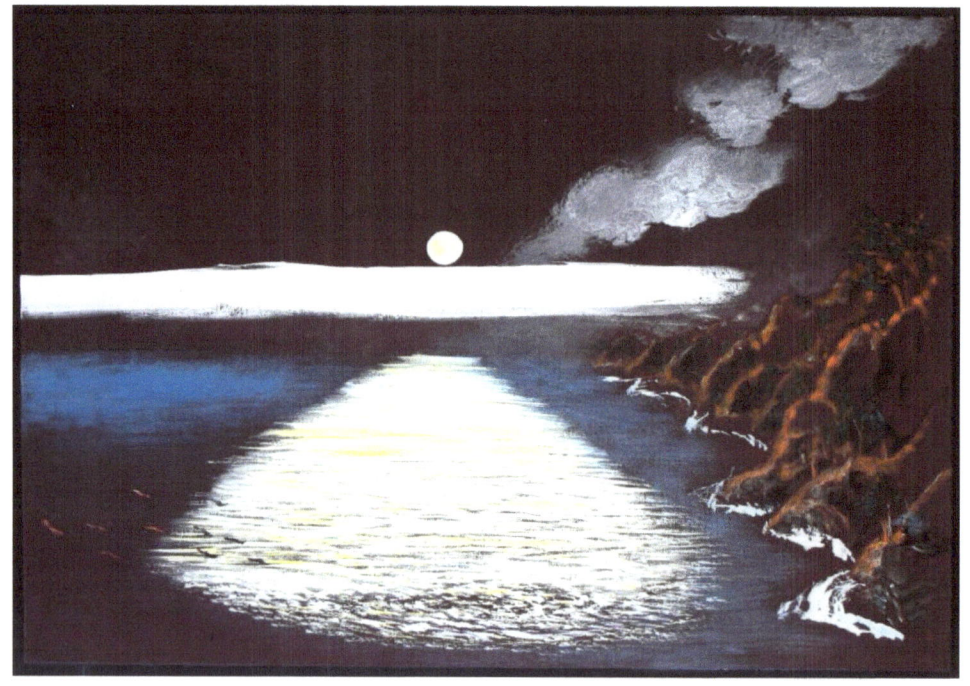

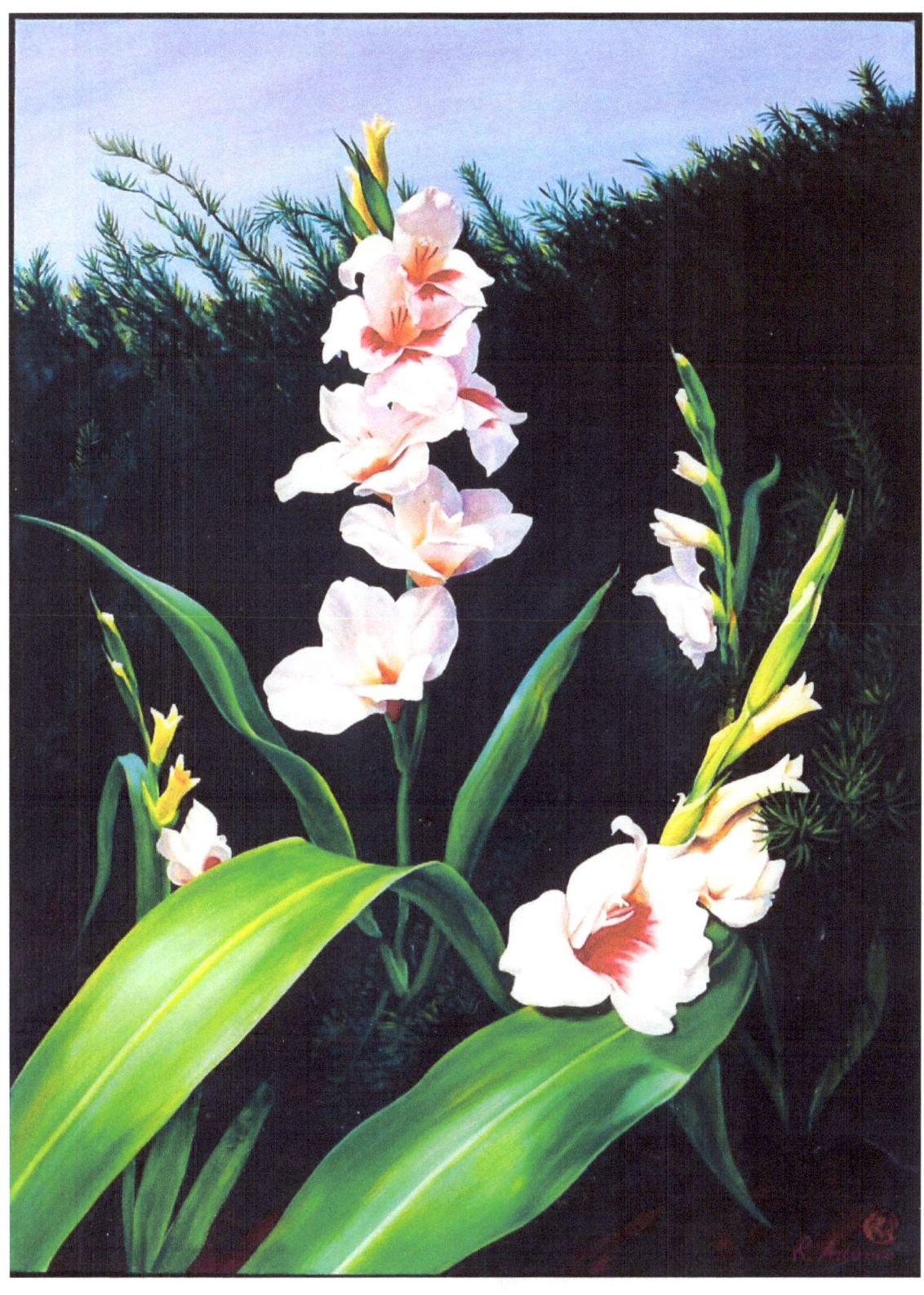

"Glad's"

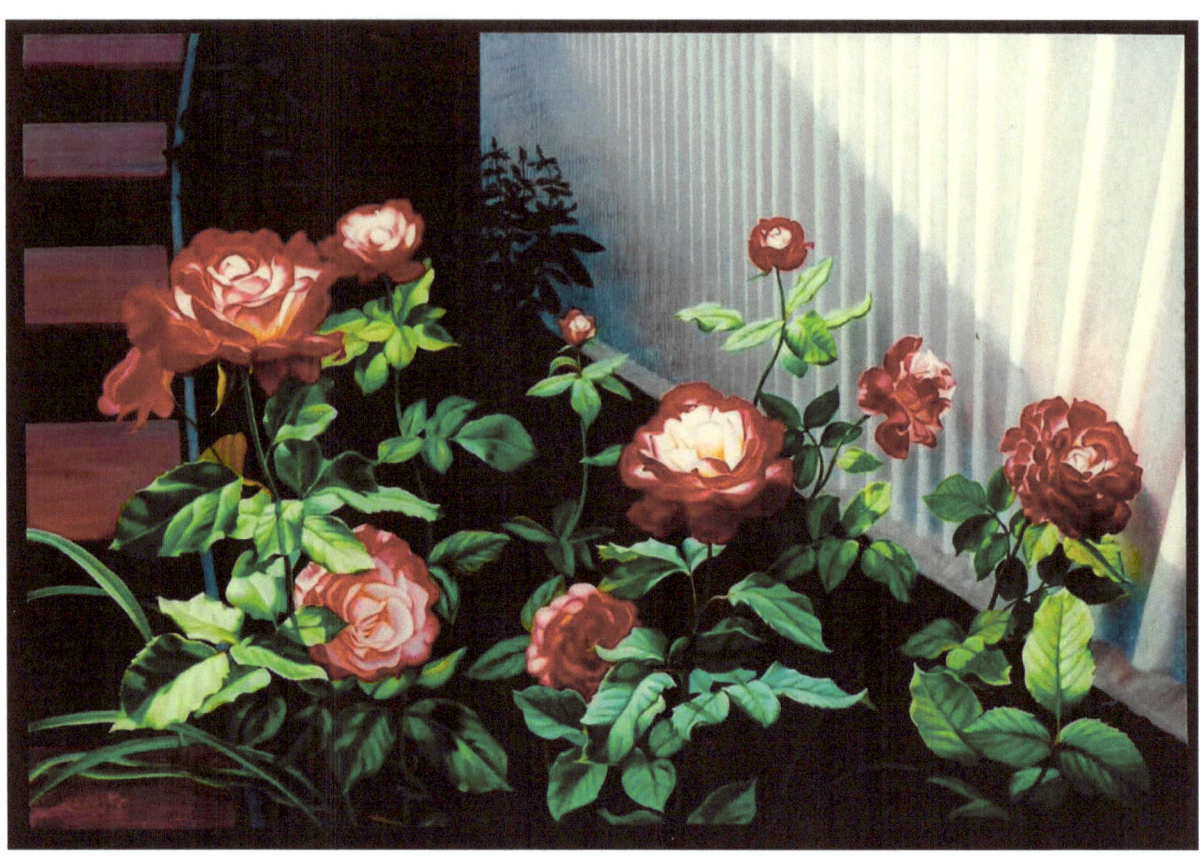

"Tea Roses"

"Rose Design"

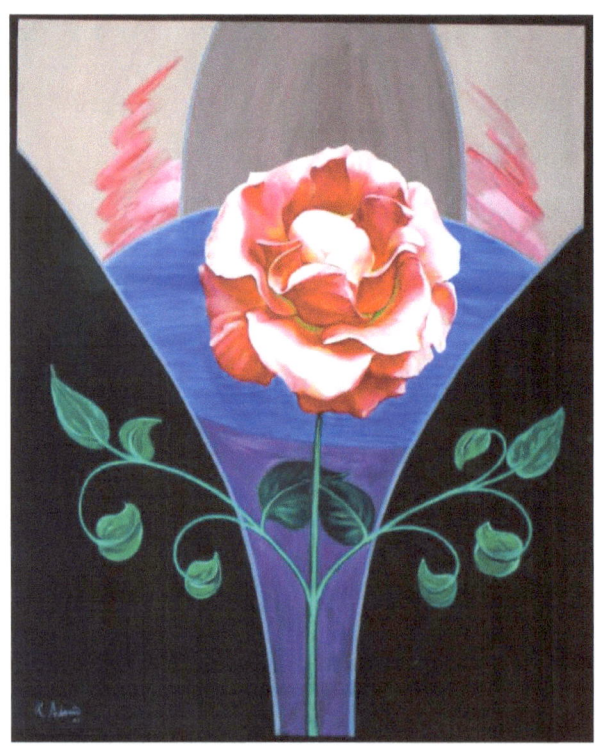

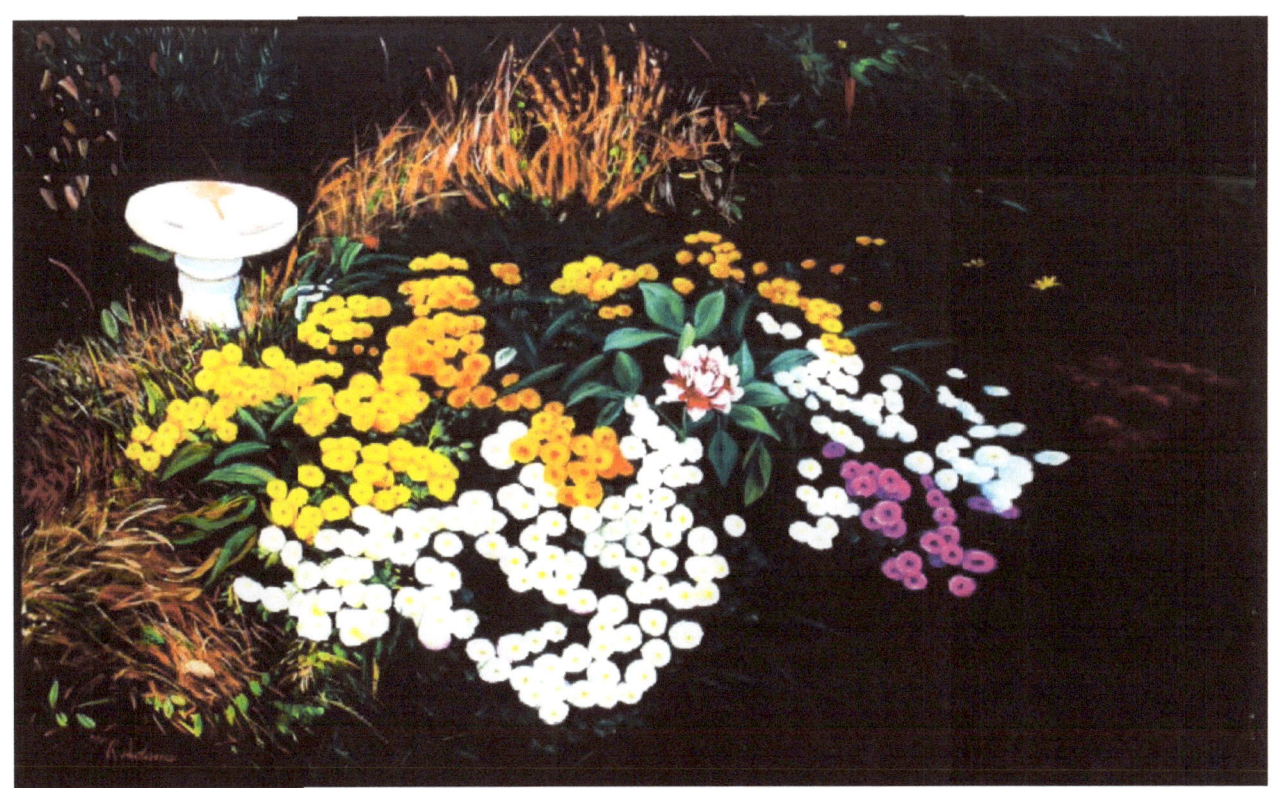

"Brilliancy 0f Burning Self"

"Chrysanthemum Garden" ("Among all the mothers of the world, alone, my mother is best.")   (- H. A.)

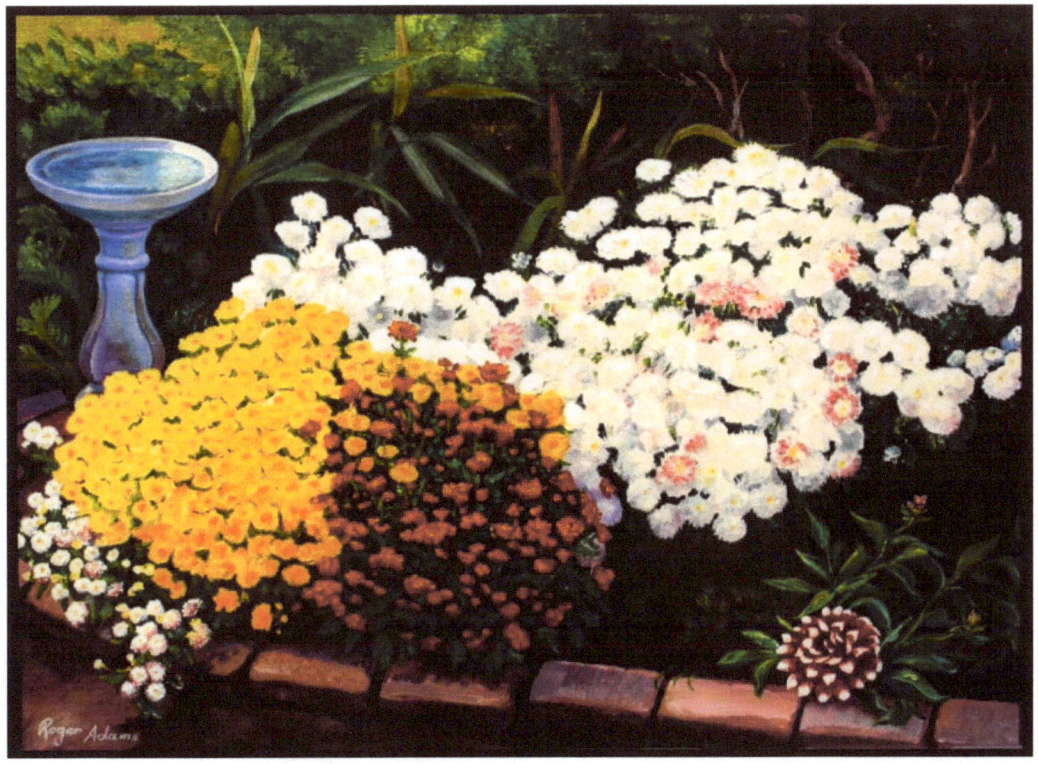

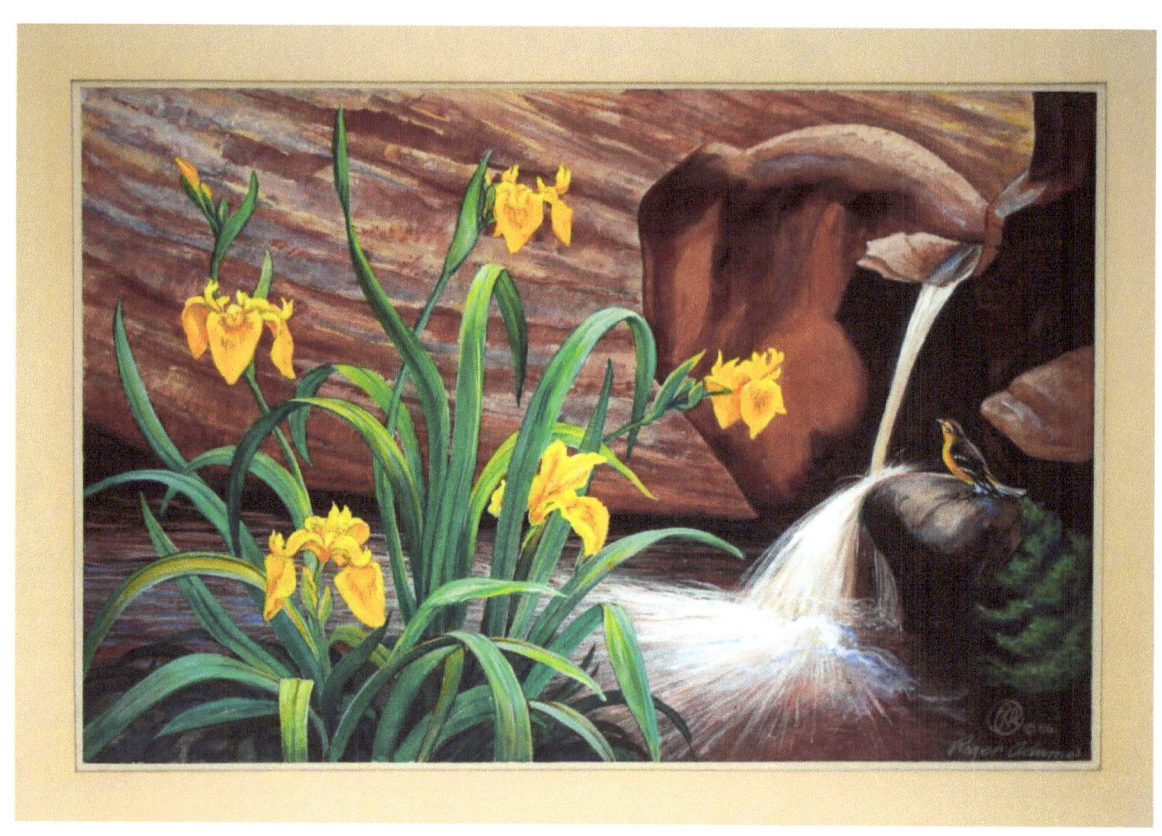

"Wild Iris"

"Park Scene"

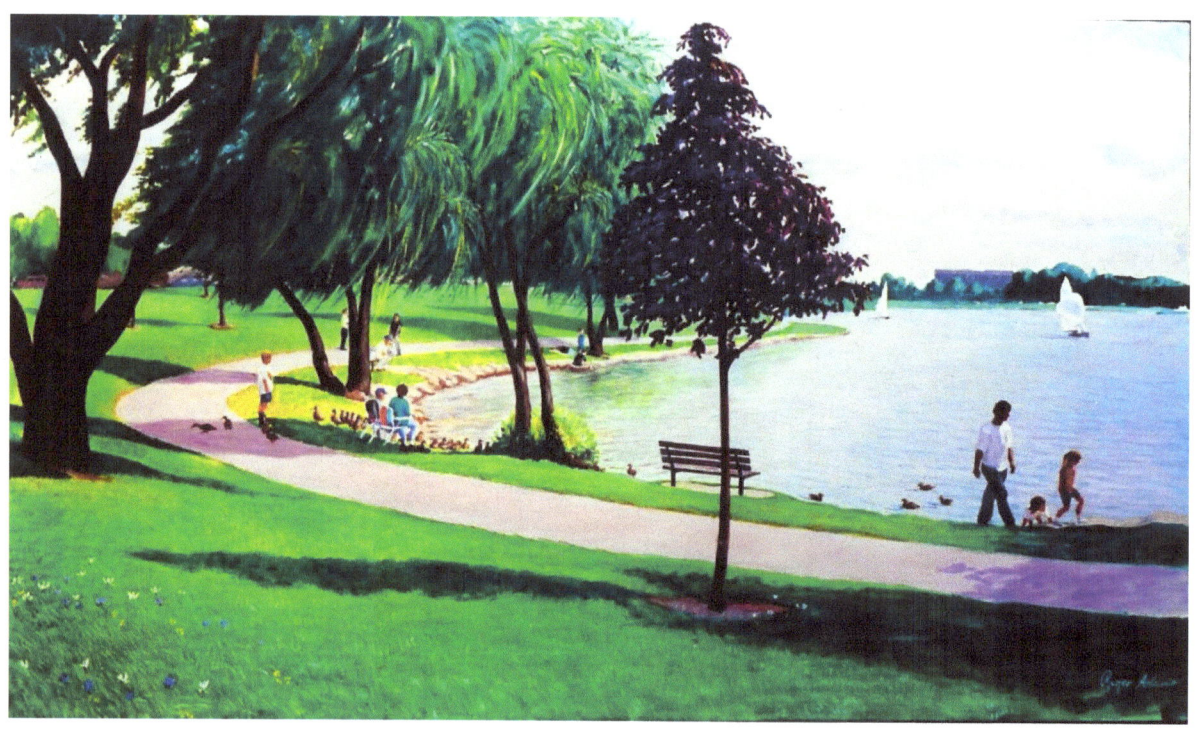

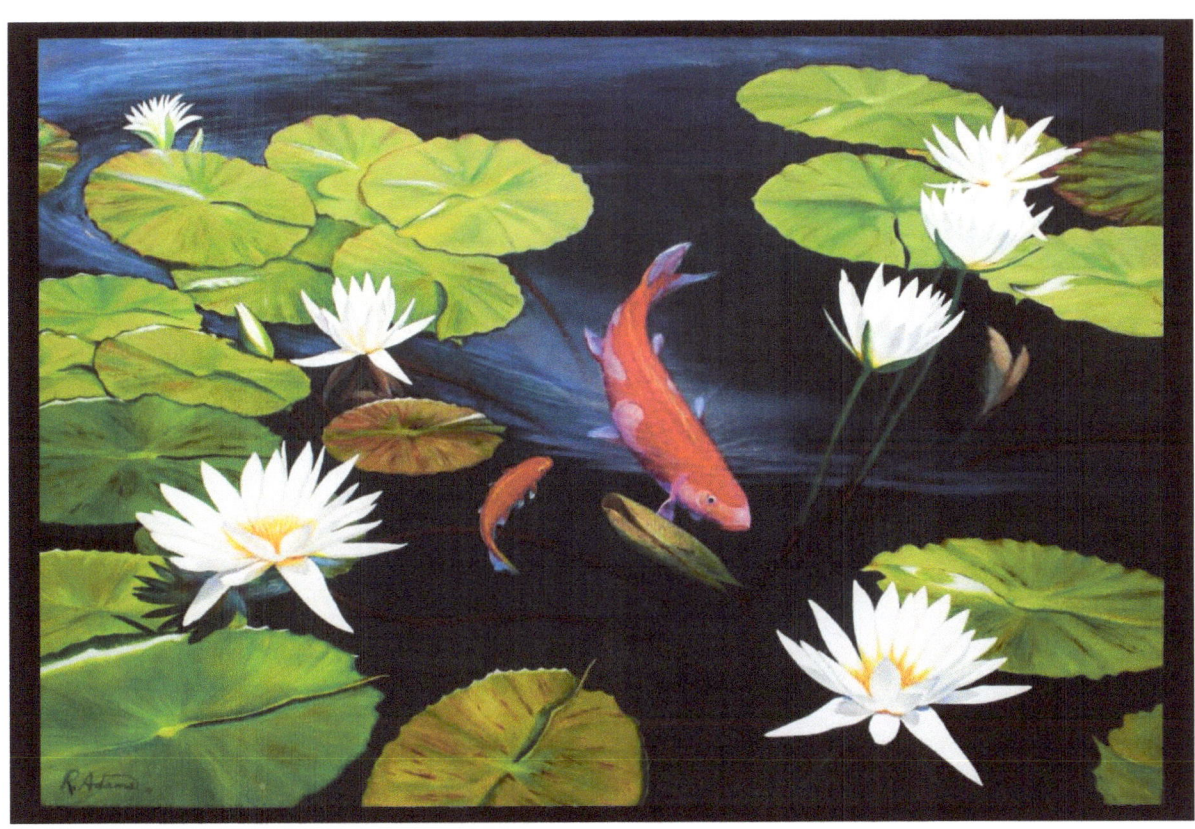

"Lotus Pond" (Student meets teacher.)

"Blooms of the Garden"

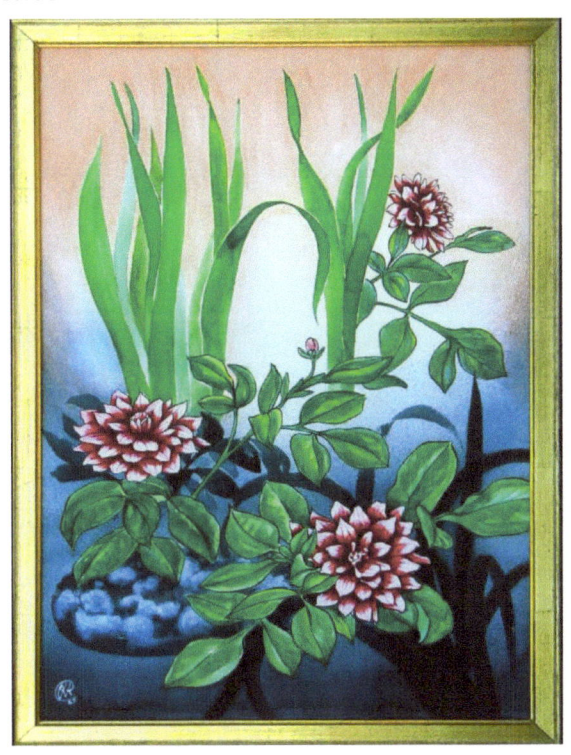

47

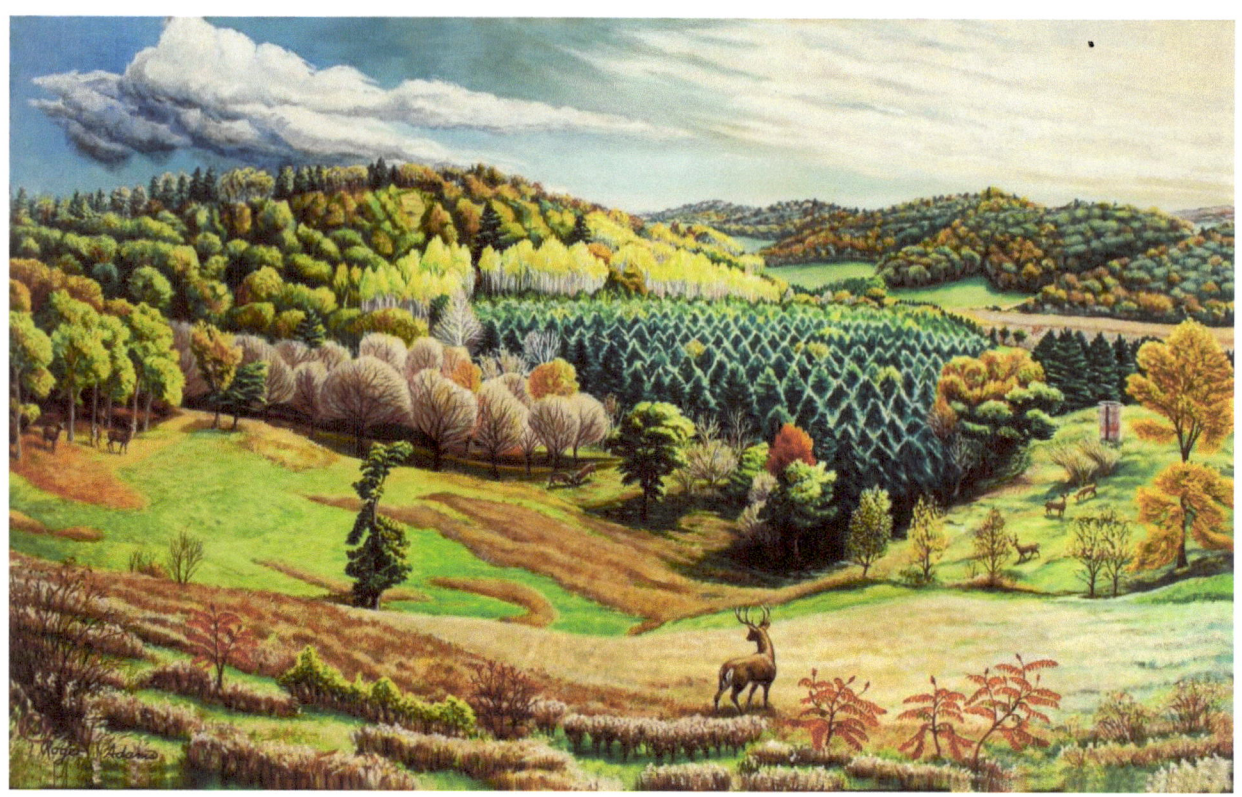

"Pure Land"

"Spring Blossom Time"

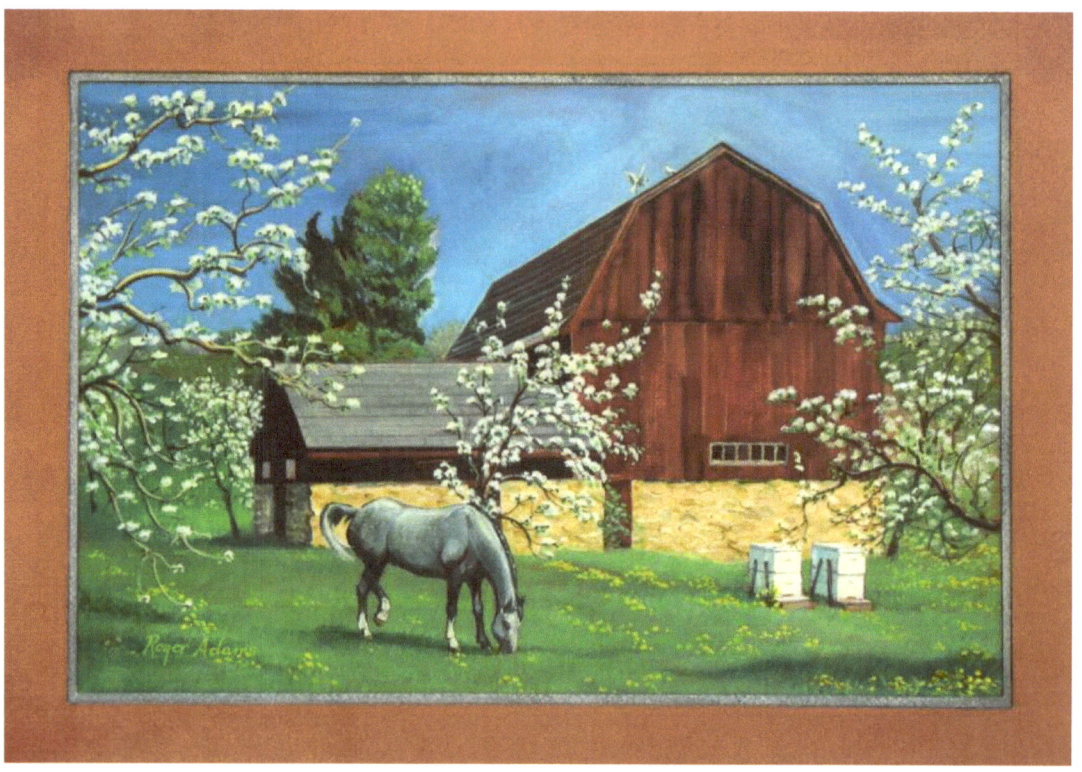

48

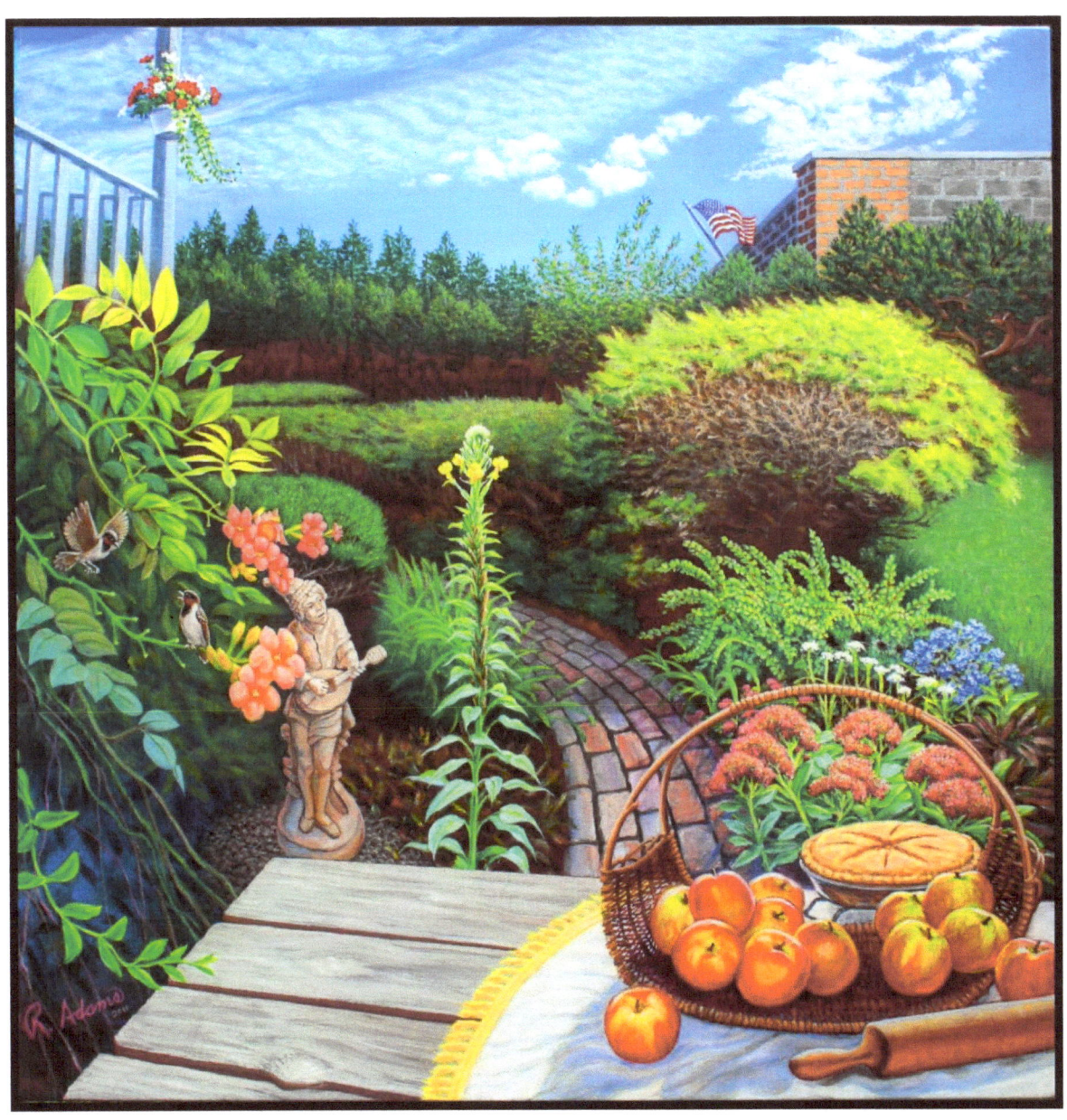

"Late Summer's Delight"

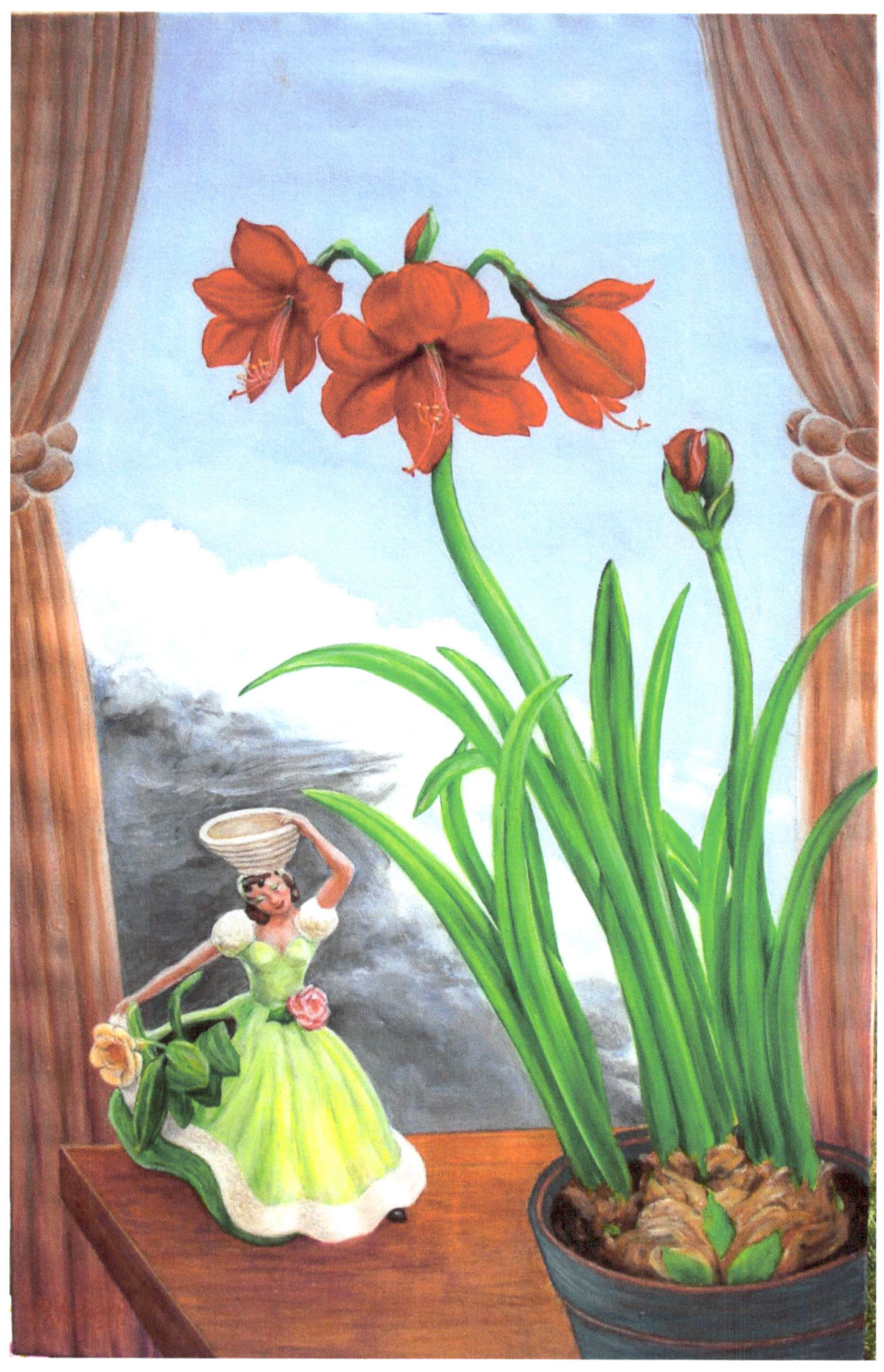

"The Amaryllis Is Dancing"

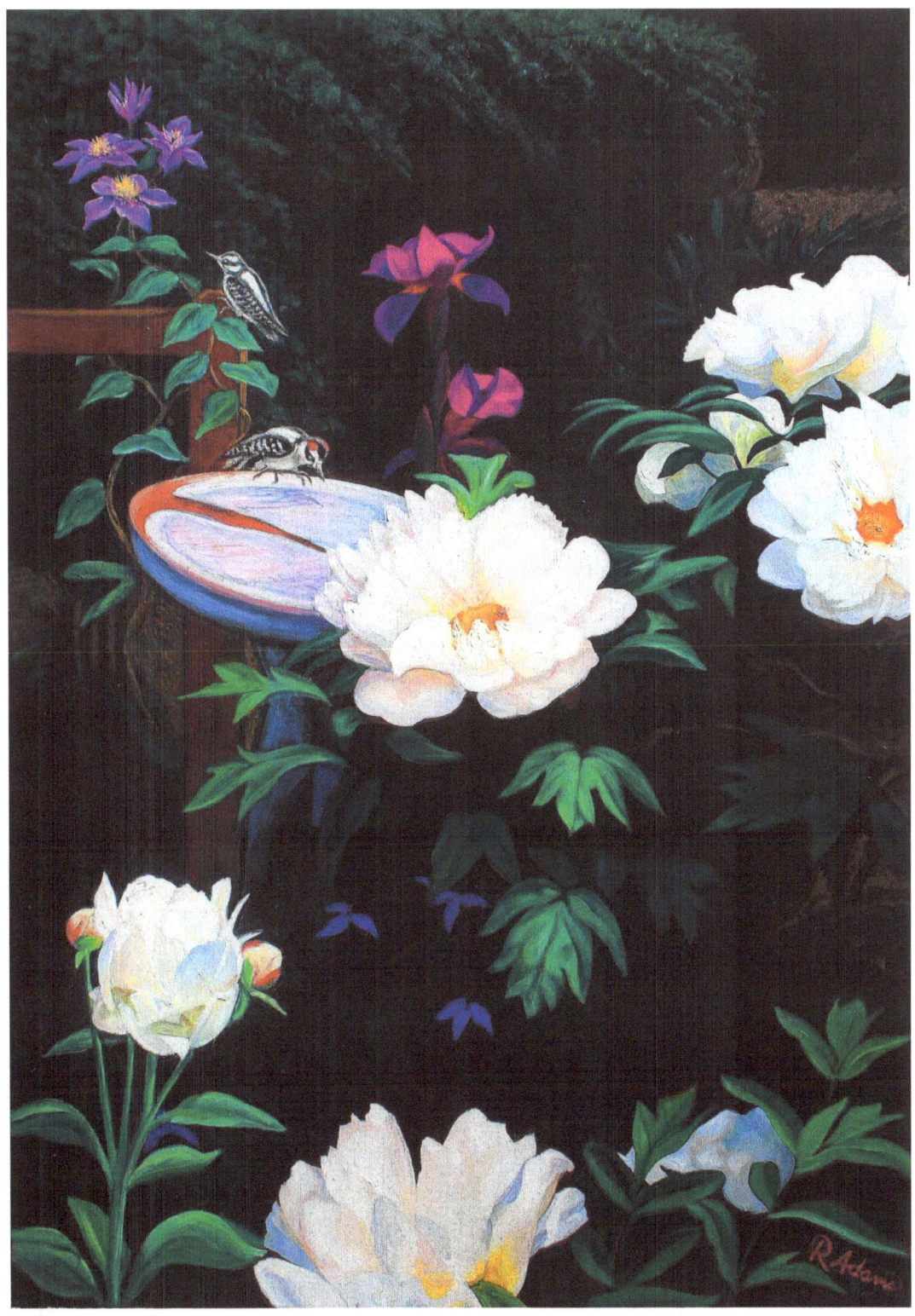

"Bush Peony"

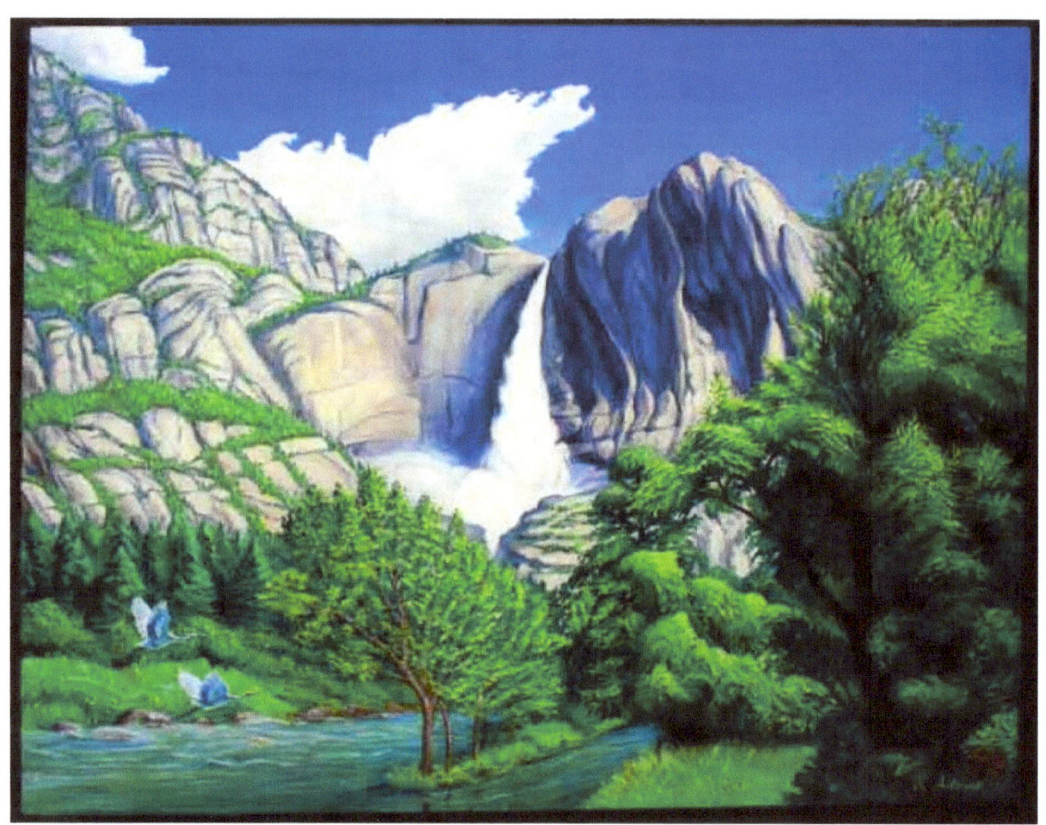

"Yellowstone National Park"

"Grand Canyon" "Eternity" "The Abyss"

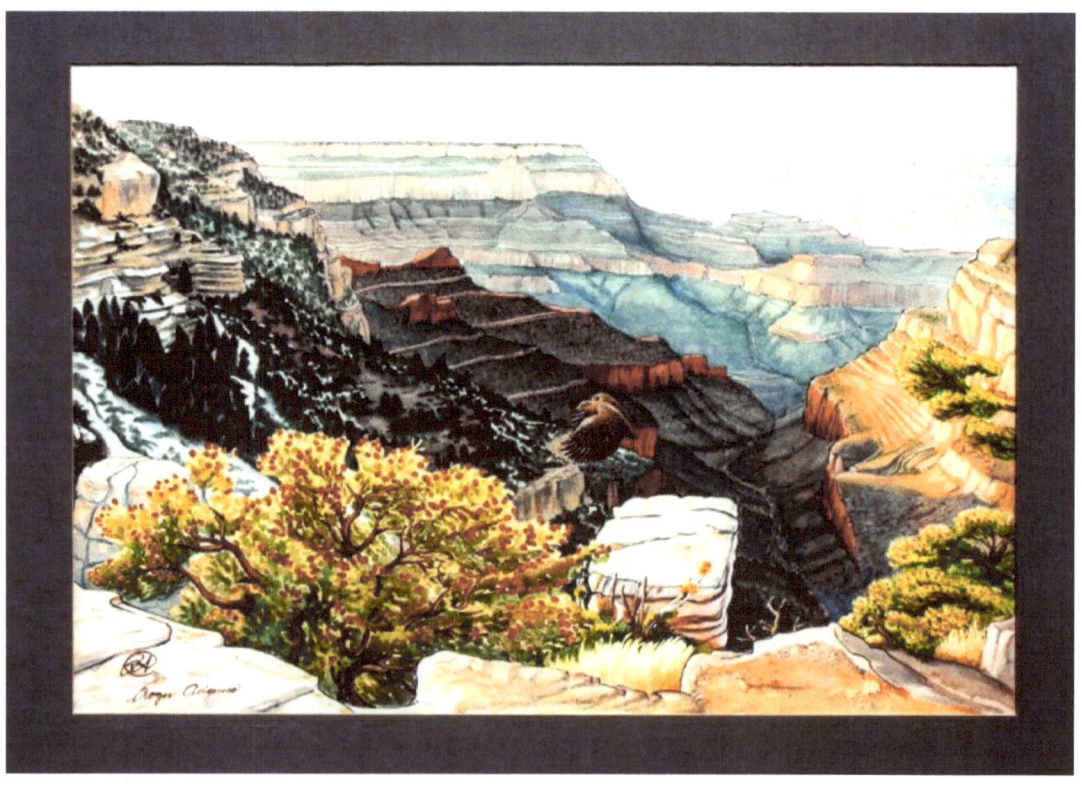

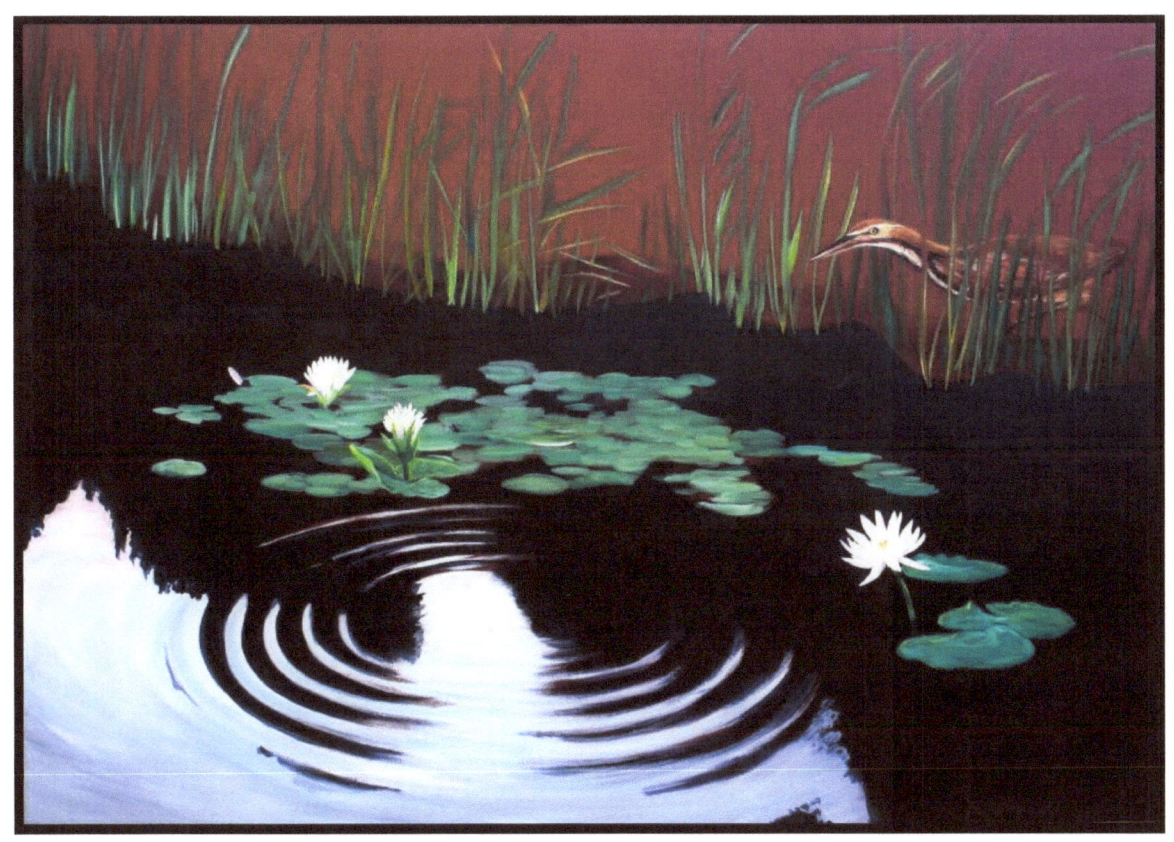

"Splash"

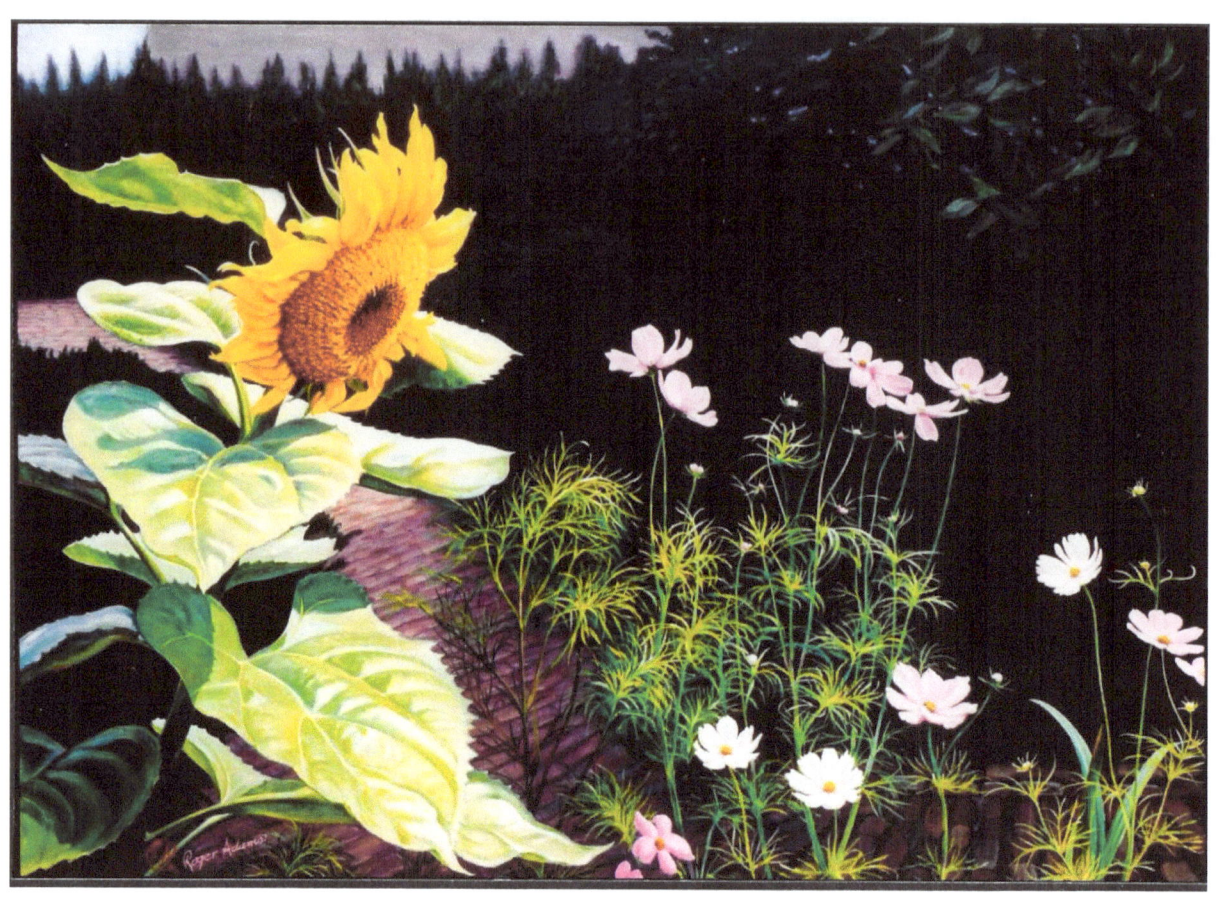

"The Cosmos"

"Snow Scene"

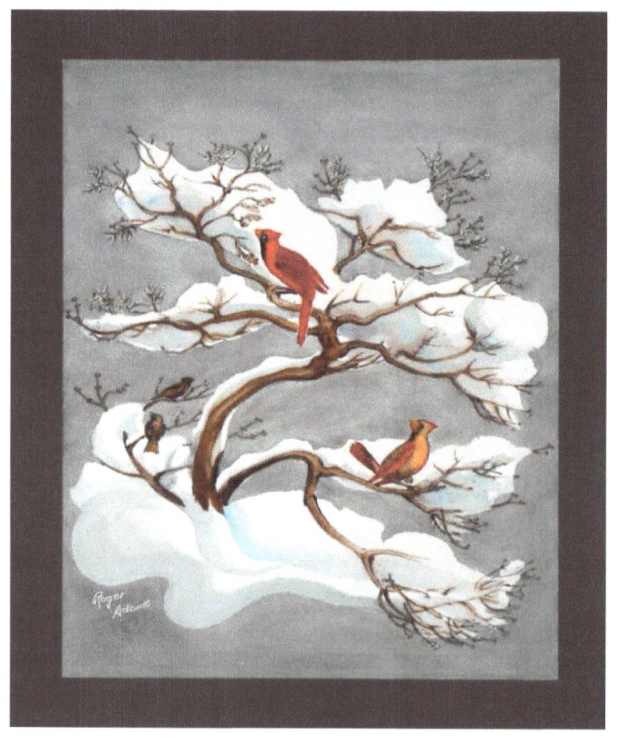

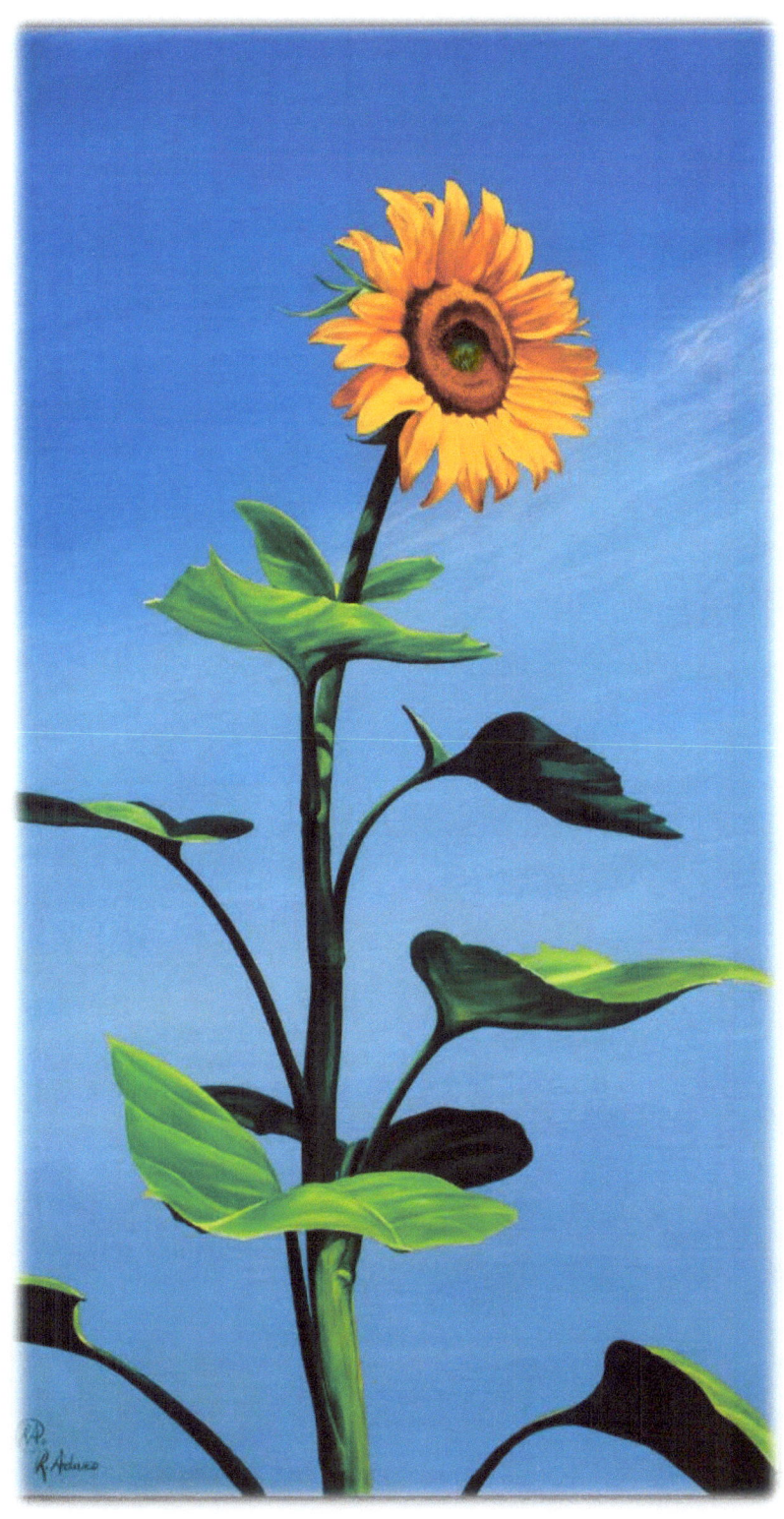

"The Yearning"

❖❖❖

   The original instinct for my coming to the Buddha-Dharma as a young man many years ago has been answered. It was this "Who am I" question that drove me to find out, this deeply buried wish to find exactly who and what I truly am, a universal question appearing in all those at a young age. Following this wish alone, I myself has been fulfilling this wish. I made it! To focus on this alone, not trying to save myself or trying to save others, but being focused only on the spirit that is my life as I am settled within my original aspiration, not needing to improve myself or trying to save myself, for the spirit within me is good enough for eternity.

   Emptiness is like the full moon in the clear night sky. The pure naked mind is the feeling of eternity, which like the moon is shining so brightly. I aspired to become a person that moves within his own environment, respecting the environment of all others who are already enlightened; just as the flowers in the garden, or great nature itself, in all its manifestations!

   Emptiness, like selflessness, which is the clear and open mind, is the recipient of all the things which in its freshness comes to me. A one-of-a-kind "onceness" that inspires life, which then inspires my wish to move forward into a world of things that I've never experienced before!

   Come as you are it says: be the sun of your own unique universe, a universe that shines on all things, enlightening all things.

   Do not be bounded by your limited self who seeks external things aside from your noble self, but seek the open spaces where you can fly and soar into the unlimited space that awaits you. Follow your original instinct, the original vow as it appears, to seek and find the original self that has unlimited possibilities into the unknown and unknowable life. We become dead when we don't touch upon this living, squiggling soul which is the rhythmical truth of our life. And in this stagnant death there is a vacuum in which evil fills, and this evil creates all kinds of ugly things. Remove this – seek into the living essence of your life – and confess one's own ignorance before life itself, and you can experience the freedom within the fresh life. This is what it means to be truly alive, and nakedly open to be at one with life itself, and that which enables you to be at one with others, while seeing yourself in them. So, self-examination and confession are the way to freedom; as blinded by ignorance, we are bounded by it.

   But, if you should stumble and fall in the process the difficulty can be overcome by such single-mindedness that allows you to push forward no matter what. The way is difficult, but the rewards are endless into our total freedom. It is the freedom to be myself, just as I am, and to share this freedom with all others so that they, too, can find their glowing jewel of inspiration into the infinite life of self-realization.

   As our understanding broadens and deepens to its fullness and well-roundedness, and I see a multitude of Buddhas grow into uncountable numbers, I cannot help but recognize the truth about ourselves is really given to us by others. In that case all others expedite my own enlightenment. And what exactly does this enlightenment consist of? It consists of being an awakened and humbled human being. I'm an ordinary person who is as being the last of the unenlightened ones. Having a naked mind brought down to zero; an emptied cup, enabling me to be open to all others, who in their teaching or help expedite my own enlightenment.

Artist of Life

Part 2

Reality is made to exist by Eternal Life. All the wondrous things happen within this eternal life, including the Tathagata of continuous change which gives me the freshness I need to inspire a new creation and to feel the freshness of the world as I begin the new day. I don't need anything other than this to enliven a spiritual life. Without this spirit there's no sparks but just a kind of existing. But when I first started out I didn't know anything about all of this. But I did have an instinct for what it was that I was seeking religiously or spiritually.

Inadvertently I became a student of this spirit when I began to realize that I was not just a person with a body wandering around aimlessly, but wanted to discover who I really am. Yes, formal education gave me certain skills, especially in terms of language and other skills in order to obtain a job, but did all these skills including jobs answer my most essential question? So in other words, the secular world had no answer for my problem. Yet, I lived in this world on a day-to-day basis, got my sustenance from it, met with others who were going about their business just as I, so what is so wrong with that? But it still doesn't answer the main question that lay buried in my mind as to, "Who am I?" Thus I left home to find out a spiritual discovery to this enigmatic question resting in the back of my mind.

While it is true that I was seeking, it is also true that I was being pushed out by some unknown power of instinct. Now that I think about it, this power that both called me and at the same time pushed me out from my parents' house was to discover a world within a new insight coming out of the Orient, mainly China or Japan that spoke of Zenism and "Enlightenment" and new ways to seek my life within the area of religion. So I had a deeper sense of what it was that inspired me.

So I prepared, left home, following the famous "Route 66", where all such people like me joined with the "hippy crowd", and went the way of such brightness all the way to California where I hoped to set up shop as a muralist and seek out a "Zen Master", or someone who was knowledgeable in oriental spirituality and wisdom. Such a youngish dream I had back in the late fifties. Then I eventually landed among the hippies – what a crowd! I got tired of them – besides, it was getting too confused, noisy and even immoral. So I found a place near the ocean, a small cabin sitting near a beach called Muir Beach backed by the beautiful Muir Forest and further on, Mt. Tammilpious. A perfect spot for Zen meditation as I was in paradise! I could watch the brilliant sun going down into the ocean. I found a cute stray puppy and then found a job as a painter. Yet, despite the fact that I was surrounded by all this beauty and naturalness, I became increasingly lonely. Something was missing. Family, friends, I began to miss them terribly. A sense of emptiness entered that I had no answer for. Besides, I'd seen the world that I wanted to experience. Thus I could not find the answer here; I must move on and come back to Chicago.

The adventure ended with my returning home with a junky car that was held together underneath with 2 x 4's and bailing wire tied to the underbelly to make sure that the car wouldn't break in half. Ha! – If I pushed the mat aside I could see the road underneath! Miracle – I returned home with .75 cents in my pocket! What a trip, the whole thing! (Those were the days before credit cards). Being back home I met with my parents who were glad to see me still intact. Next thing I had to attend to was my girlfriend who I loved and who I knew wanted to get married with me and set up a family on a small acreage somewhere in Michigan and to raise horses, and all. But I knew that if I got married with her then I couldn't pursue my wish to discover the world, cure my irresolvable skin problem (psoriasis), and meet with the "Zen Master", and etc. Marriage had to wait – pushed aside – because of my strong feeling for what I now see as my essential wish, or, "Who am I?" It was really becoming a spiritual destiny.

Now however, after a period of seven months, I was ready to get married and settle down. But she was nowhere to be found. In that sense I was ready to return to normal life. Spirituality would have to come through living a normal life. Aside from normal life there is no spirituality. Normal life is the reality of the world as it is. As Rev. Akegarasu stated, "I do not understand why Gautama Buddha did not return to his family." Once you find the essence of your being through self-recognition, then how could family life disturb your meditation, but in fact deepen it? But anyway, coming back I once again pursued my original instinct. It was now becoming something of a deepest wish.

In my mind at the time, the world was divided essentially into two parts; on one hand you had the secular world, and on the other hand you had the spiritual world. The secular world was the finite world where we as human beings were born, worked, lived our lives, and died. The other was that of the unknown or infinite. In the secular context we as finite beings played out our desires and various attachments all controlled by self, thus all our selfish desires and attachments came from here. Self-love of us is at the basis of this. Then this individual develops a distinct identity which we know as the ego, that insists on its own self-based independence. This self-affirmed ego becomes hardened into a shell-of-self. As the self hardens, we become more isolated, and as such, our life becomes so difficult.

The thing about the ego, driven as it is by self-power, is that it won't admit defeat, or guilt. Yet it is standing on the wobbly seat of evil thinking that it is worthy of recognition; or conversely, by comparing itself with others, depreciating on one's self. It thinks of itself as the center of the world, yet the center of this world is not moving; it is static, inflexible (except in the case of convenient motivation), and as such, no life. No joy, no brightness, stinginess, coldness; often becoming mundane scholars who judge others based upon their limited understanding of should and shouldn't. Thinking of themselves as good people who are morally pure and self-righteous and who are trying to force themselves to be so – but are'nt. Sentimentally loving, attached humans are so cute. See on the stage of human affairs how human beings practice their "devil-ship" on one another under such lies, cover-ups, deceits, disguises, fake-outs, subterfuges, and corrupt contrivances that you wouldn't believe!

Yet despite all this, we all yearn to be at one. Here we are expressing the human being in our almost unconscious desire to be at one with each other. This is akin to our true aspiration, isn't it? We suffer as a result of not being at one with each other and the world at large. This is so because the infinite is represented by the One alone. The infinite is not divisible, yet ever moving, ever changing – like a great wind or soft breezes – like torrents of water or a still pond – the infinite in all its descriptions is boundless. And it hits us. It is this "compassion" of the infinite that teaches us real compassion by compelling us to make our own real confession as to our absolute ignorance before life itself. It is here where we taste the real absolute; and, compelled to bow before it, we draw tears, and these hot tears melt the cold ice of our minds. <u>Now</u> we are made into humans who can experience true spirituality at one with the infinite, the eternal life that we cannot understand with our small relative knowledge.

The whole point of his being alone and naked before Eternal Life - as all the gods fled - is the birth shout of Gautama Buddha upon his awakening:

Above the heavens, and below the heavens, alone, I am most noble.

This discovery, this shout of total independence, led to the brightness of his face and smile - which out-shown even the sun, as it was likened to black ink sticks in comparison (refer to the <u>Larger Sutra)</u>. How joyous is his enlightenment, as I feel it within myself. This organic feeling gushing out from the depths of his being was the birth, not only for himself, but for its contribution to religion, and to the world.

Little did I know when I first began my journey to find out who I really am that I would be planting a seed, a seed that would sprout, grow and mature into a world to worship. Within the one self, is the One Soul of the universe. Its like the ocean with its tides of swirling confusion that represent our surface life, but within its depths represents the peace and quiet of the self-realized person. Yet both are part of one ocean. So when the Buddha returned to the world as a Bodhisattva to help all those who lived on the surface, he planted the seeds of encouragement to all those in need to transcend their smallish self-confined world, and to open up into a world that was infinitely larger, deeper, and free of the attachment to self and its difficulties, and to be selfless. The true self is decidedly selfless, which at its core is the Buddha's birth shout; the place where I can truly find who I really am, as myself.   (1/11/2017)

Early in my adulthood I sought a possible alternative to the traditional religions that were taught to me, but that I didn't respon to. Then through various means I came across Buddhism which could possibly answer the question of, "Who am I?" After all the formal education that I received, I really did not know who or what I was. Simply put, these questions lurked in the back of my mind for some time, and was pushing me to find out who or what the self is. Of course it was intuitional since I did not know exactly where I was going into this travel into the unknown.

Subsequently, after trying to locate a teacher in so many ways and travels I came across a person, a minister in a Buddhist temple who right away touched my life to the extent that I began to experience transformations going on in my mind as to what I was that allowed me to focus on the various causes of my ignorance as to the original question. He set me and others aright as to the main reason for our going around and around endlessly in a world of suffering and delusion stemming from the three poisons of greed, anger and ignorance; with no real point to it all, no real substance to who I was or where I was going. It's like living a dream within a dream. Or, like living in a house that's afire and not knowing where the fire is coming from. Attachment to the self, the un-awakened self - living in a world not knowing who he was in reality. But, earnestly seeking the truth, the living truth of the oneness within the world itself, the changing nature of existence, and the pure mind within the freshness of the Pure Land. All these things relating to Mahayana Buddhisim and beyond – all these things that enlightened my mind he exposed us to.

We all have within us this noble self. To find it we must seek into the life of Gautama Buddha who came up with his very own shout of total freedom and independence. An emancipated being – who found uncountable numbers of buddha's – so many in all of the ten directions, and fulfilled his life as a lion among men who could teach to all people: "Come to me, just as you are!"

The original question now became a vow of innermost aspiration. I must proceed to follow, listen, and hear the teaching of the Buddha-Dharma as brought forth by the teacher, Reverend Gyoko Saito, who I trusted completely. He is the main reason for who I am as I am today. His guidance and effort that he unselfishly gave to all of us is why his memory lingers in my mind; so much so, that upon his passing in 2001, I vowed to write a book exposing his life, along with my life, to give us the true nature of what the Buddhist Dharma really feels like, so that we too, can find out who we really are.

R. A. 11/10/2017

As humans we all seek the truth of ourselves and the world at large. In that sense we are no different than Shakyamuni who sought not only into himself but into the nature of existence itself; or, what is the nature of our own existence? We live within our own mind, so each person will see the truth accordingly. But the absolute living truth itself is what the Buddha discovered when he took those seven steps thinking over self- introspection, meditating on what essentially amounted to his seeing himself as a devil in the darkness of delusion: the delusion of all his self-power efforts to cleanse himself of all impurities and attain the highest level of the Pure Soul, a god-like state known as Atman. "Oh Avidia!", "Oh Darkness!" he exclaimed, as he reached his ultimate limitation, feeling so depressed and useless. In this darkness he cried out as he saw himself as being a devil. After six years of ascetic and religious practices he realized the futility of his self-efforts to attain his original goal. In the seventh year where he sat under the bodhi tree in deep meditation, he stared down Mara the Devil-King who was tempting him with all sorts of delusions of pleasures and war. He was reborn with a clear, clean mind into his decisive shout of total freedom and independence. The nobility of his aloneness; that of not having anything to depend on led to his shout: Above the heavens, and below the heavens, alone, I am most noble.

So many elevate the Buddha to the highest level and put him on a pedestal as a figure to worship, putting him way above themselves and creating a distance between themselves and the Buddha as a special person, unattainable within a lifetime, and so they seek another lifetime through a reincarnation; or, never truly fulfilling their life here, they seek another one by expecting to go to heaven upon death. All religions have these same traditions of heaven after death. Either way, they are still tied to the idea that their life will go on forever, a concept that is taught to them early in childhood by those who live in a sanctuary of so-called, "saintliness".

In back of the Buddha there was the devil, that is, his total darkness. From being this devil in darkness he emerged into the brightness of light, which removed this darkness, transforming, by the reality of this light, into an Ordinary person, able to communicate with all others by looking up at them, not down – as would someone who considered himself as someone special. In other words, he didn't see himself as the Buddha, it was others who named him so. He returned to the world to mingle with the suffering people of the world as a beggar carrying a begging bowl under his cloak – which, by the way, was made out cloth discarded from a crematoria site, washed and sown together to make into a cloak. Being possession-less is a matter of the mind itself, and how the mind is unattached to things of this world as well as unattached to himself is what Shakyamuni practiced, and because of this way of life he was a person of freedom of the spirit to travel and go to wherever his spirit led him. I think of him as a person of nothingness, of emptiness that entered the buddha-lands that were established after he died, enabling and enlightening all those millions of people who followed him and heard his teachings. In that sense he was very approachable both as a student and a teacher.

My teacher, Reverend Gyoko Saito, had a dream soon after he came to this country (which I've shortened) in which he was sitting in front of his teacher, Reverend Haya Akegarasu, who in a stern voice told him: "Just promoting Buddhism is not much. It is only when Saito truly becomes Saito; when "I" becomes, "I as I", then you will touch upon the very core of your life as the truth gushes out as your very own shout." When he awoke he was in tears.

As I was a student of his for forty years I can verify the words in this dream as coming from a person who really lived it, and being totally involved with his life, these thoughts, these words become my words as well. Neither a layman nor a monk, in the ordinary simplicity of life, I can pursue the endless teachings of the enlightened ones, who themselves came up with their own life, independently.

Through the purple clouds of darkness comes the shining light of the Buddha's wisdom.

A formation of geese are heading south for the winter,
their voices calling sharply in the high, open sky.

Winter is upon us giving us super cold temperatures and good amounts of snow. These are the prospects we face now as it's already here. Tomorrow will be shoveling day, and right now I don't mind. I have prepared and have everything I need. I have nothing to think about as all my thoughts lead to nothingness. Right now, there is this atmosphere of emptiness where I am free of concerns and responsibilities, enjoying life just as in suchness, or "*isness*". Yes, that of *isness!*

So often we think that something is important for our survival and so we take on the responsibility doing what is necessary our survival. I don't care whatever it is we get involved with; all kinds of twists and turns of thinking our way through survival so that we don't get thrown out into the street – how terrible or impossible is that thought! Face it, we are the most attached ones when it comes to the death of ourselves, including all of our possessions.

No use talking to people about how free the Buddha was in his no-possession life. We have, on the other hand, possessions that we highly value. Our home is number one. Then comes everything in it and so forth; including our cars and favorite clothes, and etc. Yet all these things that we possess can and do put a heavy burden on our shoulders as we try to maintain them. I too, feel the same way as to all the things I've accumulated for years and years, plus all the things that my parents left me in that I don't know what to do with it all! It can become a real problem. Why so? And if so, what is the solution?

We pass over nothingness, well, because it's nothing. But ironically, as we think this way can we in the end, survive? It sounds paradoxical but because of a fixed way of our conventional thinking about something, nothingness exists to deny it. We are clearly attached to a fixed self. We love ourselves. This seems perfectly natural until we introspect carefully about what this self-love has in the way of consequences to our cherished life-style. Everything seems to be in the way – all kinds of stones that are constantly popping up in an otherwise smoothly flowing river of life. In this way the very self is the one that clings to all that we claim as our own, to be causing a troubling and discordant agitation in our mind. The cause of all things going on in the mind is through subjective self-love. Therefore, as we go about seeking a resolution to all of our problems we seek a solution that appears to be easy, fast, and ultimately cheap – in other words, we go for cheap solutions. These solutions can be delusional and unsubstantiated by the reality that we really face. Therefore, and accordingly, since the fixed notion of self-love (ego) seems to be the one causing all the trouble, why not be selfless to the extent of getting rid of the self and become selfless? If we can have a pure self that is "selfless", why not? That sounds perfectly logical till we attempt by our own power to get rid of that bad self. Now, however, we are faced with a conundrum, a puzzle which can't be resolved by our relative thinking. It's like using a dirty eraser to clean-up a dirty spot on a sheet of paper. All we will be doing is smearing it around. These are the conventional methods we so often rely on to resolve our difficulties. But they don't work, and we are left with a continuation of our original problem. It is like the dirty and delusional self is trying to clean-up the dirty and delusional self. This is the impossibility that Shakyamuni faced and that we all face in turn. We try to purify ourselves using an impure self to do it. This is so typical of the way one's secular way of thinking goes about fixing an impure self.

Selflessness is like emptiness, a spiritual direction in which we have no control over. It cannot be controlled by the self. It cannot be controlled by prayer, and it can't be controlled by ritualized procedures as authorized teachings; that which we normally think of as good religious practices.

Nor can so much sitting meditation practices, yoga practices, dietary restrictions, drug use, or any number of practices that are used to quiet our unsettled mind. All artificial attempts only sidetrack us into thinking that we can control our uncontrollable mind. Our mind keeps churning around and around endlessly anyway, despite our best efforts to quell it. Some latch onto anything and everything, to gain their self-centered and pleasure seeking life-style. What a miserable life we can lead as a result of our misdirection's and the blindness of not knowing the truth.

Selflessness comes from a power beyond the self, which in a sense, is a gift. Think of it as a gift because it cannot be arrived at by any method derived by self-power in the way of seeking it. It simply comes to us after we truly realize the utter futility, stupidity, and uselessness of all our self-power attempts. Finding myself to be a totally useless person who was guilty of improperly understanding the teacher; and who, upon his funeral, totally broke down into uncontrollable tears…. is my confession. Otherwise, I was dealing with abstractions and concepts that were really outside of my life. Truth came to my understanding by way of the flesh, not by way of concepts. A concept is only a concept, it is not actual life, as life itself is not a theory.

Beyond the intellect and its resources, is the Power Beyond Self (or Other Power); a power beyond man, the spirit of which transforms our identity from fixed to open, from hardened into subtle, and from a noisy, restless person into a well-settled quiet person. This constitutes one's true religion beyond all the rest of our attempts at good religious practices, even though they seem as a reasonable contribution and preparation for our eventual awakening. But, only when one's innermost aspiration is deeply aroused do we enter into a trust of non-retrogression.

Here we have touched upon the core of the Buddhist teaching: a power beyond the self. This power, is the wisdom of the Buddha's teaching (as evidenced by his being a mendicant monk as a beggar) is through non-attachment to worldly things and the worldly life. It is the life where attachment to the relative self (or surface self) is burned up within the extinction of a self that is useless and has no idea as to the workings of the compassionate and amazing power that we ourselves have no control over. The compassion of an unknowable source that has no name or form, yet has the power to move us and create a transformation within ourselves. It supports us and embraces us like a mother to a child. In other words, we are supported by a power that we don't even know about. But, once we do, we place all our trust in it.

R. A. 12/12/2016

It is here where the essence or figure of Amida Buddha comes in. The Larger Sutra focuses on a monk by the name of Dharmakara [storehouse of knowledge] who has as his aspiration to become a Buddha just like his teacher, Lokesvaharaja [king of the free life]. He bows to him repeatedly while praising him, then promises to fulfill forty eight vows that he completes, acquiring the name of the Bowing Buddha, or Amida Buddha. This is the basis for a particular sect of Mahayana Pure Land Buddhism called Shinshu Buddhism, the true faith sect.

Amida Buddha being as its focus, it is divided into two parts, both parts being immeasurable. Namu Amida Butsu is the chanted version of bowing before the Tathagata of Infinite Light, and Infinite Life, the focus of which is Amida Buddha. Infinite Light (wisdom) and Infinite Life (compassion) are the contents of Amida Buddha of which we must aspire to become. A symbol, not a God, Amida is not aside from me. It is an indispensable requirement for the trust I place on the Power Beyond Self. Here I am as a servant unto the master, the master being Eternal Life. By placing one's total trust in this alone, we are saved into the compassion of an all-encompassing aspiration, and will definitely be assured of attainment of Amida's perfected wisdom and compassion. This is the original intent of Buddha for all people to keep in their heart and mind.

This was the victory that Shakyamuni attained as well as was his survival, for he was nothing but skin and bones as a result of extreme yoga, dietary, and ascetic practices; which as we noted previously were to no avail. His final attachment was to self, the final attachment we all face and that which we must abandon if we are to see the light of the Buddha's wisdom. But why is this so important? The self must survive at all costs no matter what, and it is here where we fear death the most. Because of this we will be bothered by all kinds of problems, some reaching into the extreme. But, if we do not fear this death, we will no longer be worried and disturbed about the smallish things concerning the smallish self. We can then focus on the immediacy of the present moment-to-moment life with actional intuition: i. e., by seeing we act, and by acting we see.

Upon his enlightenment the Buddha lived as a Bodhisattva; and within his teaching, was playful. His return to the world as a Bodhisattva in this case is not the traditional way. Observing my teacher over a period of time, he had a unique way of displaying his playfulness, in subtle ways too. He never took on the serious face of a person who thinks he knows something; the conceited person, a snob, thinking he has such-and-such knowledge and being so satisfied with it.

So selflessness is the way to freedom, and our deepest confession is the way to get there – not controlled by the self – but by the uncontrollable feeling of tears that we have no control over at all. This is the power beyond self that finally we face-to-face meet with.

R. A. 12/13/2016

The sun is out after four days of cloudy skies and so much snow. I've cleared it all away, such a big job. Now comes the bitter sub-zero temperatures.

Inside, the sun is reflecting on all things, bringing life to all the indoor plants and those that have buds and are getting ready to bloom in time for Christmas or New Year, like the Christmas cactus, for instance. Whether it is the sun, the plants, or my being itself, all things are coming alive, being embraced by the feeling of openness and a sense of oneness. I am delighted in this atmosphere of enlightened beings which bring me to this home base of flowing with the river of life itself.

That which I can control and that which I cannot control are two components of the world and of the mind. We worry so much about things that are out of our control. We can divide these two things into internal and external. What can we do about the external things that are aside from our actual life itself? We sweat over things that we have no business sweating over. I can't control another person's life, but I can help them concern for themselves. We like to practice all kinds of goody, goody things. We drag ourselves down by the amount of time we devote to nonsense. Our life will not go on forever, let's spend our time in focusing on that which is significant to our heart/mind as we truly live and fulfill our life.

My spirit is dancing, and within these movements there is no inside or outside in opposition to each other, but rather they come together as one – unborn (buds), birth (flowers), and rebirth, being a Buddha seeking Buddhahood, or the past as fertilizer for present and future life. All things – so much of the Pure Land experience is intertwined with one another by subjectively resulting in a spirit within the mind of *isness*. The living material coming from the work it takes to create from a base that inspires me to express my life through my own art. This is what it means to be an artist of life in the true sense of the word. It is your life you communicate, isn't it?

With this I can communicate with all others in the sense of a genuine dialogue; equally, respecting the others' right of independence as well as my own. And this dialogue continues further to apply one's resources to every aspect of life and within it contains endless possibilities for the life of creation, touching the cosmos itself.

The very idea of infinite life came from the Buddha and our ancient ancestors, our Pure Land masters, the Seven Patriarchs; the 7th which was Honen (1133-1212). Later, his student Shinran Shonin (1173-1263), the one who founded Jodo Shinshu Buddhism [true faith sect], and his emphasis on Amida Buddha, by the power of nembutsu in transforming one's secularized mind that is dead into a fully living person who has a spiritual direction and focus. Thus, transforming the nature of our ignorance into the shining light of self-realization, or Shinjin (Awakening).

This enlightened feeling effects not only my life, but all others, transforming everything into the living truth organically, where pure subjectivity within the mind of one who flows along the great river of life into the vast ocean where everything mingles together as one. Samsara (world of birth-and-death), and Nirvana (self-extinction or selflessness) are as one, participating in this continuous-discontinuous movement forward into the unknown and unknowable depths of the ocean wherein all things blend together to form the taste of the ocean. The ocean holds no dead bodies, all blend in as one taste. So, Samsara is Nirvana and Nirvana is Samsara, blended as one.

Even though these words are coming from myself they are essentially in their essence at least, coming from all the modern and contemporary thinkers from the East. This would include my teacher; all those who have given us such essential teachings that inspire and motivate my efforts to expose them to the world. The teaching we should really study and contemplate so that we can live our lives as true human beings. This spacious world! This transcendental *isness!*

Once we catch this instinct we can be a true artist of life, practicing our art on a daily basis; in no matter what form it takes with a youthful mind of exploration into the depths of our life in the process of discovering it; from the authoring of these articles and book, entitled: "Artist of Life – Festival of Youth".

Roger Adams 12/14/2016

THE SHINING LIGHT DHARMA

The Dharma refers to the Buddha's Teaching. It comes along with the Three Treasures: The Buddha, The Dharma, and the Sangha; the Sangha being the students and followers of the Buddha-Dharma.

There are many kinds of dharma's (teachings) in the world. These are given by wise people and sages, and by those who engage in relative wisdom's that apply to some people and not to others, and so they are limited as to their perspectives and opinions. But the Buddha-Dharma is universal in that it is applying to all people.

The Buddha focused on the self, since it was the self that we must examine in order to determine who we really are in actuality. Wanting to know the self is why we come to Buddhism to learn who we are as individuals, not merely to think we know our selves but to penetrate much deeper to find out who and what we are in reality, and to flow along with the continuous change that occurs within all of life itself. All of our ignorance, delusions, and vanities are seen as blockages to that freedom that we wish to experience. With this freedom comes peace and happiness which is so essential to our life. This is known as enlightenment or awakening – the experience of shinjin – a transforming experience into self-realization.

How interesting are these teaching's, that open our mind to the wondrous world that is taking place all around us. We may be unaware to see it this way. As we live in our own mind, so will we see the world. The world itself begins with my own life and is not aside from the living essence of who I am. This living essence feeling the sparks of life, and being at one with all of life that is the joy of being at one with the shining light of the Buddha-Dharma, the Tathagata.

> The symphony of light;
> Amida Buddha's life of compassion –
> The Tathagata of change burning up all evils.

Shinjin – from here, all our negatives become positives as we awaken to the true spirit of our life. How amazing it is. The struggle of seeking, the difficulty of understanding; and, the victory of transcending the difficulty we have with others, and particularly within ourselves. It gives, on the positive side, an incentive that pushes us further into the unknowable truth that is beyond reading, writing, and study…. leaving us naked before life itself. That which is on this shore of the pursuit of one's own happiness so often ends in suffering, leaving us to seek into Buddha's wisdom, which is to seek into the reality of truth as to ourselves living in a secular expectancy.

From this shore of the secular world we try to imagine what the other shore is like. Across the turbulent river of fire and water representing water as our greed, and fire our anger for not getting what our greed desires. We, with utmost tcourage, must cross over to get to the other shore. The most positive life is to be found here, as is a well-settled feeling of true happiness going forward with one's own honestly lived life. How fulfilling it is, engaged in returning to the world to help awaken all the lonely, suffering people of the world.   R. A.   12/21/2016

Wormwood

Poems by Reiman Tsukamoto

Ah, wormwood leaf,
    what a longing for –
Do you know how much
    I have longing for you?
Do you know how I thought
    when I found you?
I wonder what you thought
    of me when you saw me.
You have been buried under
    ice during the long winter time.

How you really survived not
    being frozen to death.
You may say – I will blossom year
    after year like this year.
But how deeply I long for
    such an ancestor of your life.

                (1917)

Reiman Tsukamoto was one of those early Japanese immigrants who came to this country in order to get an education and then go back to his country to establish his life.

At the time of his coming here America was entering W.W. 1 and he had to enter the draft. Not wishing to do this he became a conscientious objector and went to Alaska. In so doing he, at the same time, threw away his future.

During his life I understand he worked in a fishing and also had other jobs. But people say of him that he became a Bodhisattva in that he transcended this world of desires.

People who knew him casually did not know his real talent for poetry, nor did they suspect what a deep person he was.

His attitude towards nature is somewhat based on the "I – Thou" relationship, yet without the "thou" becoming capitalized as in the case of Martin Buber, who made the I – thou into a kind of God-like relationship, -- or thou became the God. Such a crystalized form of God comes about when the thou assumes a static position.

For him, Tsukamoto, this wormwood shrub growing in the wilds of Alaska symbolizes his organic relationship with all beings, it is not just another weed growing. But it is the first leaf that comes up in the first awakening in spring.

It is really something to try to understand how he feels and how much a value this wormwood has for his life.

This "ancestor", this "ancestor of your life", -- what does this mean? What is he really looking at or into? I don't think he is seeking for merely a leaf, but something far deeper. Undoubtedly he is in a special time and place and his longing for life is such that the transition between the long winter and the first buds of spring have such a sharp meaning. One feels that the plant is talking to him, -- like a girlfriend, like. I wonder.

Translated by Reverend G. Saito, 1980.

In reading this poem I am put in such a deep mood. The "ancient ancestor" Reiman refers to makes me think of a poem-like writing by Reverend Haya Akegarasu in which he states: "I go to the unimaginable one", the ancient ancestor of an unknowable source of life. How can I understand this? Truly, it is beyond my limited understanding, that is, my limited understanding cannot penetrate into the depths where these words and feelings are coming from – no amount of thinking will supply an adequate answer. No amount of philosophical sophistication, study, scholarship and learning will even touch upon a world that, in itself, is beyond description and/or conventional logic and thinking, no matter how much we try.

Words must come from reality – real experience – at the very moment they are uttered. These are living words, not mere abstractions. If not, they become only abstract concepts with no life to them, and certainly no real meaning touching the core of my life. They cannot move us. Therefore, in meditating and thinking about this subject I have to go back and reflect on the substance that these words imply, which means that you have to go back to them repeatedly to gather this deep meaning within yourself so that you may be at one with what is being said.

The poem is speaking to me directly the sense of Eternal Life, as a gift to the author; in such simple of terms, shedding away all the external stuff.

So, in our whole list of words that can be used to translate unfathomable expressions that will deepen the difficulty, even confusing one's surface mind and understanding, so that it can be brought to light, the light of our true understanding. It is here where we meet with such words as One Soul, and, Feeling is <u>All</u>.

An organic essence permeates the mind of a true artist of life in which a person transcends the duality and separation between himself and the other, and his or her expressions will reflect upon this fact. Here, fact means reality, the reality of our true religion, and spiritual essence.

"How difficult it is to be a true human being." my teacher said on several occasions. He is referring to the spiritual life that makes us truly human, as otherwise we are without our depth.

From an old letter I received from Joan Sweany, is an article which she and Rev. Saito translated some years earlier from Reverend Haya Akegarasu's writings. A partial excerpt:

"... But when I am sitting quietly by myself, I feel such a warm communion with others, such gaiety! – a longing, yet such a cheerful mood! Without reading and writing, hearing or speaking, I melt into that rhythm of nature which cannot be read or written heard or spoken. Then I shed tears, and I smile. Out of the depth of tears, the miraculous spring comes forth.

I know all beings in the lonely self and taste communion in this loneliness. It is not enough to say I am thankful or reverent – these words do not express my mind. As I walk I bow my head, and my eyes move with the rhythm of nature that flows under my feet. Tears form and fall; the blood dances in my veins. I go to the unimaginable One."

Our ancient ancestors in Shinshu Pure Land Buddhism – so far back into the past - which includes Shinran Shonin (12th cent.), who wrote these following words of absolute trust:

> I take refuge in the inconceivable light.
> I rely upon the Tathagata of immeasurable life.

This is the essence of Amida Buddha we can aspire to become, and it is this that makes us truly human. Why is it so important? Because it makes us humble listeners, learners, and practitioners. If we are not made humble we cannot hear the truth. The quiet person, the truly humble person awaits for that living truth that comes to him even while not seeking it. This is the miraculous spring that suddenly comes to life as manifested in Akegarasu's poem.

Because he follows the way, the truth is given to him expeditiously and in accord with great nature's flowing essence. This is our ancient ancestor we most carefully listen to. We, like servants unto the master, the master being Eternal Life. So we can't afford to be careless, sloppy, and indolently lazy persons; disrespectful towards our own life and the lives of others. If we are not humble, diligent, with our mind that is open and awakened, how can we expect to feel the true spirit and immortality of our life? It is something to really think about as we re-read the simple poem by Reinan Tsukamoto and the article by Haya Akegarasu.

The truth is within our creative life. It is also within emptiness, the nakedness we feel when all the external and worldly things are removed. When the secular world no longer attracts us we are freed from its ugly side. When all I see is its ugliness then I am freed of all attachments to it by simply following the way. In following the way, we can feel the flat ordinariness of the quiet person, who like others, lives in the world of birth-and-death, and yet is not attached to it.

How majestic, how beautiful and joyous that are the result in simply hearing the words of my ancient ancestors. Oh emptiness! Oh creation! And, may the oldest be the youngest!

> Amidst city noises
> the peony bush blooms,
> capturing me instantly.

We, the ordinary work-a-day people providing our best effort for all those around us, can give light and life to all those we meet. All of us can be our own founder of a truly democratic way of thinking, based on listening to others in an open-minded way and respecting each others' right of independence. In this dialogue so many buddha's come to life! And in this dialogue we can feel ourselves bowing in truth with the Nembutsu [Namu Amida Butsu]. This feeling is the answer to the ancient question of who am I, not aside from Shakyamuni the Buddha, the ancestor for us all.

Then there are the Six Paramitas: first, of giving (generosity), morality (right morality), listening (hearing), perseverance (total effort), meditation (self-examination), and wisdom, as listed in the Larger Sutra. The first five are method teachings, but the sixth one is the wisdom teaching that leads to our awakening. And in this awakening we bring our noble spirit to life.

As we gather all these Paramitas we will find our way through the difficulties we face, even as they are likened to poison; to find the truth within ourselves of the modern and ancient teachers in a way that shines through my life, as the deeper we go the more treasures we find.

Addendum

I need your support. I will appreciate any support you give me including your referral wherein you can express your thoughts and feelings as to this book. Let's continue forward into the Buddha-Dharma where we can all participate.

To submit reviews on Amazon a customer must make a significant amount of valid debit or credit card purchases ($50. or more) if you are not a customer on Amazon. But, if you are already a subscriber to Amazon's *Prime* you're good to go. Customer support: 866-280 4331.

To submit a review:
1. Go to the Amazon link, www.amazon.com. In the search bar type in <u>books:</u> and then type in the full title of the book you wish to give me a referral on. Click on the book. Scroll down till you find <u>Customer Reviews</u> located at the very bottom of the <u>Product Details</u> section.
2. Then give me your review and click submit. I'll thank you.

∾ঙ   ∾ঙ   ∾ঙ

The Light of Hope

From the darkness of our mind comes the light of hope. Isn't it beautiful? The start of a new life. The new life is filled with hope. This hope is the brightness which is so quiet. It's just hope itself - out of nowhere it comes. There's nothing except this naked feeling in dispelling all else.

I don't expect anything out of this hope. It's like a dance. The spirit dancing to a song of unknown origin. So too, is the shining and enlightening quality of hope that transcends darkness.

It's being with good friends wherein a dialogue of communication leaves me with such a warmth of mind. And from this mind, comes the light of hope. All life shines with it. All life comes with it. It is the most ancient ancestor we can meet with. For it begins with the creation of all things since time immemorial. Its effulgent dimension cuts through the bondage of self.

We must live, and we must die - die to the old useless ego-self - birth of a new self just like a seed bursting through its shell, being born with such sparks of life and a hope that shines within. Effort it takes, effort to come to the point in our life wherein hope endures over all else.

----

www.theshininglightdharma.com.

AUSTIN GARDENS BUDDHIST CENTER

A JOURNEY INTO THE BUDDHIST DHARMA

Two books are offered for sale at amazon.com; or at createspace.com, (an adjunct of Amazon).

1. **The Artist of Life – Festival of Youth:** 79 pages. Thirty three pages of informative text, plus 61 full color prints of my own paintings and artwork. This book is also available in a Kindle or eBook version only through amazon.com; as it is not available through createspace .com, which publishes only physical copies.

2. **The Shining Light:** The basic Book of 257 pages: "A Journey of Life: The Buddha's Teaching".

Continuing a Legacy:

With the brightness of my teachers smile I wrote these books. I knew him for almost forty years, having met him in 1963 until he passed away in 2001. In that time he became my best friend. As he was the best student he was also the best teacher, and so he became the most trusted person who could guide me and others whenever we needed his help. To have absolute trust in another person requires that you have to listen and feel reprimanded when the occasion warrants it, and so it is very important to listen to what he says and pay great attention even when it crushes one's dishonest, wrongful, ignorant, and arrogant assertions. For he never patted us on the back saying how good we were. We had to reflect on what it was that caused us to suffer from our own stupidity that prevents us from a free and enlightened condition that comes from within our mind as to not being able to see it clearly, until we make an honest confession. Within one's deepest confession, we are truly humbled and set free.

The job of the teacher was to open our eyes as to what we really were; but he did it in such a way using expedient means, that allowed us to see it for ourselves so that we ourselves could see with a humbled mind into the difficulties of our understanding. He never preached to us as if standing above us; as if he were the teacher and we were his students, so that he could teach to us in a dualistic fashion as two separate parties. As we never felt such a separation between him and us, I felt, heard, and participated in the most unusual exchanges going on that now I want to expose to the world with these two books that I've written and self-published. Through these books I've focused on the most basic teaching of the spiritual direction of Buddhism as relates to the experience, thought and feeling of the author of "The Shining Light" and the "Artist of Life" books, dedicated to the memory of Reverend Gyoko Saito, who was the teacher for all of us.

You may purchase any one of these books either through amazon.com or by createspace.com. Please consider ordering through createspace, because it allows more royalty for this non-for-profit Center, which makes my continuing effort possible in furthering the Buddha-Dharma for all.

Go to my website: www.theshininglightdharma.com for ordering books and more information.

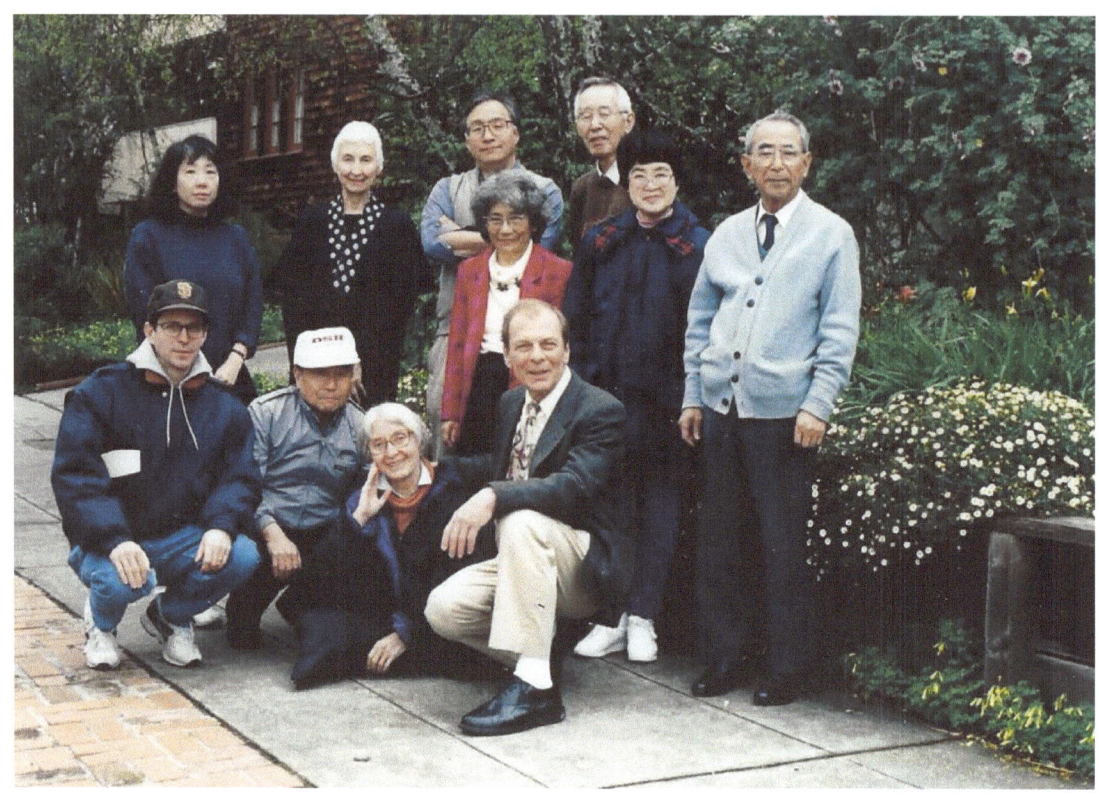

One of the first seminars at the "The Maida Center of Buddhism" established by Rev. Nobuo Haneda in Berkeley California in 1996 showing a group of us enjoying a break between sessions.

Reverend Saito is to the far right with his wife Toshiko next to him. Right above her is a visitor from Japan who was a student of Rev. Maida, and next to him is its founder, Rev. Haneda. And next to him is Loraine Black who was a member of our discussion group back in Chicago. Next to her is Tomulko, wife of Rev. Haneda.

Down below is myself and right next to me is Joan Sweany, again from our discussion group and Rev. Saito's secretary back in Chicago. Above me is Anna Nagata from Chicago, and so forth...

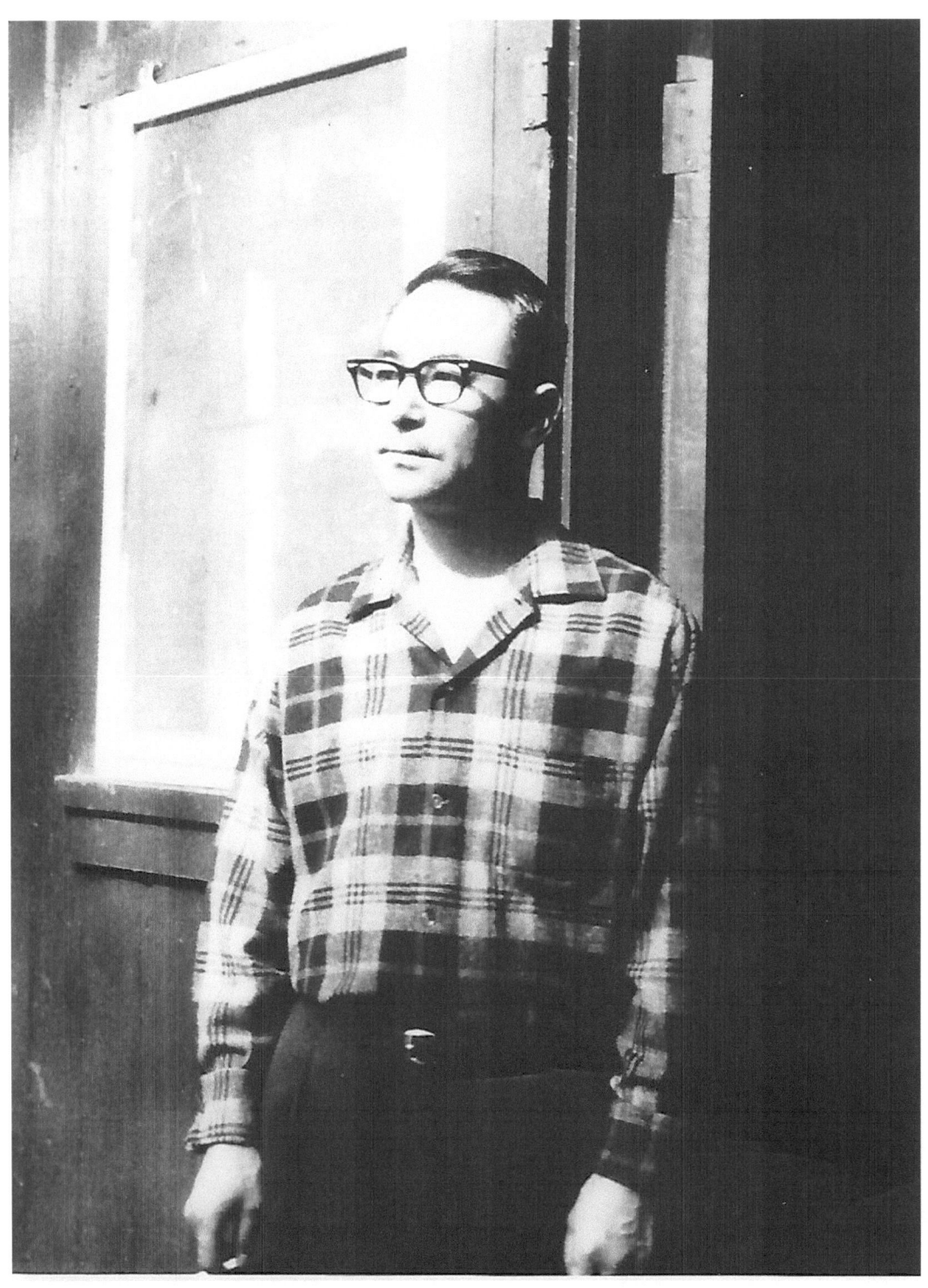

An early photo in 1968 I took of Reverend Saito who was at that time leading our discussion group under his auspices. Here he is depicted in one of our earliest annual retreats held in one of the Park Forest Preserve sights where we all gathered to participate in day long, night long discussions face to face with each other... while the teacher who knelt on the floor with a pillow under his knees giving every one the "red carpet" treatment. It got to be pretty intense at times with each of us having to describe our lives individually, but it provided an insight into who and what we are.